RADICAL LEARNING FOR LIBERATION 2

Edited by

Brid Connolly | Ted Fleming | David McCormack | Anne Ryan

First Published 2007 by
Maynooth Adult and Community Education
MACE

© MACE

ISBN: 0901519332
978 0 901519 33 7

Cover Design by Language, Dublin
Layout design and printing by First Impression, Dublin

Contents

Introduction

In 1996 the Centre for Adult and Community Education at St. Patrick's College Maynooth published *Radical Learning for Liberation* (MACE, 1996) stating that it would be the first in a series of publications mapping the development of and supporting the progression of radical thinking, practice and policy work in adult education. The Centre saw itself as part of the community of adult education workers and learners and wanted to nurture a critical debate about theory, practice and research with the practical intent of realising the radical potential of adult education to make changes in society. Though this intent has not changed so much else has.

Both the status of the university as the National University of Ireland Maynooth and the status of the Department of Adult and Community Education have been achieved in that time. In addition, a number of publications have been published in the Maynooth Adult and Community Education Occasional Series including *College Knowledge: Power, Policy and the Mature Student Experience at University* (1998); *Women and Education in Ireland, Vols 1&2* (1999); *Unsettling the Horses: Interrogating Adult Education Perspectives* (2004) as well as the most recent *Researching and Writing your Thesis* (2006). The launch of the first professional doctorate (EdD) in adult education marks the arrival of adult education as a discipline in the academy. In the past year the Centre for Research in Adult Learning and Education has been founded in the department and one of its early ventures has been to look to the contributors of the first *Radical Learning for Liberation* and seek to update contributions from the authors.

At a national level the Irish Government has adopted lifelong learning as its educational policy and published the first *White Paper on Adult Education* in 2000. The discourse in the field has changed too. Access and accessibility for mature students in higher education, though not achieved, is moving towards becoming the norm. Increasing numbers of graduates continue to work towards the enhancement of teaching and learning opportunities for adults. The priority and enhanced funding for literacy is a major change. Funding brings with it the two edged sword of acceptance and co-option. Recognition for what we do is wonderful. We appreciate and take pride in being recognised as the essential ingredient in lifelong learning. But our sharply honed suspicions are alive to the dangers of having increased state scrutiny and increased emphasis that what we do should have economic benefits. In an increasingly bureaucratic world of quality control, qualification frameworks, business plans, measurable outcomes we are not only suspicious in the way that Foucault would recognise, we are also increasingly a part of the way economic imperatives colonise pedagogic thinking and practices. Aims and objectives, outcomes, learning as quantifiable, modules of learning and compartmentalised digestible amounts are all ideas coming to haunt us from the globalised economy that seems to have an insatiable appetite for better qualified, skilled and flexible workers. Society, and the vision that sees adult education having a social agenda, are at risk.

There is more to learning than being a worker, or a consumer or a client. Becoming a citizen involves learning and citizenship is different to being a worker or part of the economy. That the state has caved in to the demands of the economy for skilled labour and in the process defined citizen as client, customer, consumer or reduced the care system to counting the numbers of trolleys in a hospital puts the onus on adult educators to constantly argue for the importance of learning that is needed for active engagement in society. We do need to learn how to live together in peace, justice and with care for each other. Social justice, care and the understanding, insight and skills needed to develop communities and families that will sustain healthy, caring and engaged citizens are at the core of the social agenda.

The Maynooth Adult and Community Education (MACE) Occasional Series is an attempt to speak of these ideas and theories that underpin our practise. It is hoped that the Series will contribute to strengthening good practice by providing a forum for critical debate. This volume is concerned with the theme of liberation particularly for those marginalised in our society. The emphasis is on a radical quest for really useful knowledge, critical intelligence and transformative social change. The new Centre for Research in Adult Learning and Education wants to further our understanding of teaching and learning and so has been instrumental in establishing a national research association: Irish Research Association for Adult and Community Education.

In putting together this collection the Centre for Research in Adult Learning and Education wanted to invite again the original contributors to *Radical Learning for Liberation* and explore the issues that now occupy their adult education imagination. Power is exercised by powerful elites in society. This exercise of power is done by promoting systems of ideas which are 'beyond question', 'obviously true', and even 'self evident.' When questioned these great truths turn out to be false. Mezirow, in the tradition of Freire, clearly justifies the superiority of critical conscientization or transformative learning as against the uncritical discourse of conventional wisdom. Originally, Jack Mezirow contributed the paper he read at a conference in Maynooth in 1995 and this volume includes that article and an update outlining recent developments in the theory of transformative learning. As transformation theory has become one of the foundation theories for understanding adult learning it is timely to present the outline of the theory and 'a progress report' on recent developments.

Jane Thompson contributed to a conference in 1996 and in the original publication outlined a provocative concept of 'really useful knowledge.' As with Mezirow's paper it contributed significantly to the development of a set of ideas, concepts and a vocabulary for adult educators in Ireland. Thompson now returns with an equally provocative piece challenging the UK Labour government's policies on adult education. We in Ireland have not escaped the debasing of the concept of active citizenship by our own right-wing government and it is stimulating to see articulated a vision of adult education that challenges the way the UK (and by implication, Ireland) use adult education to micro-manage the potentially troublesome attitudes of the lower social orders. 'And with corporate capitalism in charge on a global scale…there is little room for grand narratives, and every encouragement for the belief that because you can't change the world, you must strive to change yourself.' The individualism that underpins this vision is ruthlessly exposed by Thompson.

During the past decade many visitors came and exchanged supporting and stimulating ideas with us. Jim Crowther has been constant in this collegial work and in the process of achieving departmental status we were eloquently supported by John Field and Maria Slowey. We include in this volume two papers from the colloquium in 2002 that discussed 'The Role of Adult Education in the University.' Richard Taylor asks and answers whether adult education is a discipline in the university. He outlines the changes that have taken place in the configuration of disciplines in universities including the acceptance of computer science, environmental sciences, peace studies, and women's' studies. The definition in the university of the meaning of discipline has changed. Adult education is part of this trend partly because of its interdisciplinarity and applied nature. In the new disciplines the mode of production of knowledge has changed particularly in the way it is linked to organisations and cultures outside the university. He locates adult education in the context of the wider discipline of education while at the same time identifying the key divergences especially the pedagogical practices of small group work, common purpose aims and especially the role of the experience brought to the classroom by adults. He concludes by making the provocative assertion that adult education is the core and catalyst from which the new higher education may emerge.

Lyn Tett of Edinburgh University was a participant in the symposium too and in this contribution outlines how important it is to enhance our 'working with civil society.' The challenge for a strengthened democracy is to discover processes that can reconcile the valuing of difference with the need for shared understanding and agreement about public purpose that dissolves prejudice and discrimination. People's interests therefore need to be represented in public debates both in terms of their cultural conditions and their material class interests.

This approach is based on the notion of adult and community education as a *'dissenting vocation'* that takes the side of ordinary people against the ideological and economic forces that seek to dominate, oppress and exploit them. Members of communities would then be perceived as active citizens making demands for change with their different ways of knowing and understanding the world being valued as a resource for learning. Rather than seeking to minimise risk, the academy should be 'educating desire' through challenging and supporting people in civil society to define and solve their problems for themselves.

By inviting the Maynooth staff who contributed to the first volume to share their current research and writing the Centre for Research is providing a forum for indigenous adult educators to speak of the ideas and theories that underline our practice. These are in various ways concerned with the theme of liberation particularly for those on the margins of our society.

Ted Fleming's contribution explores the controversial idea that there may be a biological base for human behaviour. In looking at the way nature and nurture work together he identifies significant connections between one's earliest attachments and how students and teachers make meaning and act in learning situations. The radical intent here is similar to that of Fromm (*The Sane Society*) who theorised the key connections between individual and social liberation. This paper studies the ways in which culture and society are reproduced through childrearing practices and unconscious dynamics between parent and infant. The intent here is to alert adult educators of the implications of these ideas for what we do in teaching and learning.

David McCormack reinterprets the well-known academic practice of supervisors who demand a reflexive approach from their students. He turns the research gaze towards the researcher themselves. One cannot do research reflexively unless one also interrogates the researcher. This is difficult and this elusive self is pursued through the fascinating story of Lazy Ozzie. This article models the process known as autoethnography.

In her chapter on critical pedagogy Brid Connolly interrogates neo-liberalism and how it co-ops popular movements, such as community development. She sees a critical adult and community education as an antidote as well as central to the education process of building a communitarian model of community development thus enabling people to develop a critical analysis of neo-liberal development. In particular, she links critical pedagogy, praxis, and consciousness raising.

Education plays a key role in determining one's life chances and as 'education matters' a great deal to people we need to attend to the ways in which exclusions arise. Anne Ryan maps the exclusions from education and clearly identifies the system as part of the problem. The essence of the radical approach to participation in education is to change the system.

The final contribution from Anne Murphy explores how learning actually happens in the workplace. The current debates take place in the context of the techno-rational discourses of HE policy concerning formal and non-formal learning. The debates are not in tune with how learning takes place in the workplace and she explores the assumptions that are made by these discourses. New ways of recognising and validating knowledge production and learning in the workplace are required to take into account this reality.

Radical is a word that has been devalued by the right. This volume is an attempt to keep the radical alive in the field of adult education so that the commitment to change in society is not lost but fed and interrogated by this collection of articles which is concerned with the centrality of this concept in our thinking, practice and research.

Ted Fleming

Adult Education and Empowerment for Individual and Community Development

JACK MEZIROW
COLUMBIA UNIVERSITY

Adult Education and Empowerment for Individual and Community Development

JACK MEZIROW
COLUMBIA UNIVERSITY

We live in a frightening time of crisis, in a high risk society, a world turning away from a commitment to find agreement across cultures in favour of vicious, senseless terror; of rampant religious fundamentalism breeding suicidal killers of innocent people; of unpronounceable cults with messianic masters proclaiming the end is here and determined to take us with them; of primitive tribalism and murderous ethnic cleansing; of a form of global economics that enriches absentee owners and exploits the poor, in which most workers are deprived of job security or hope for a rewarding career; of rampaging reactionary politicians who would deny government a legitimate function to protect the weak, support social programs or to regulate industry; of phoney popular movements created to influence public policy; of the sometimes legal bribery of public officials by special interest groups; of hypocritical smothering of human rights concerns by democratic governments in favour of economic gains, of a democratic public sphere reduced to television talk shows, negative commercials and opinion polls; of clandestine sales of nuclear bomb elements to evil tin pot dictators; of a bloated and entrenched military hell bent to resist reductions in its budgets; of ecological disturbances and pollution, uncontrollable population growth and biogenetic threats; and of unprecedented risks implicit in new technologies like computerization and television.

For adult educators, the question is how to help learners cope with a frightening, fast changing world. A major problem is that learners cannot know what they need to know to deal with such a high-risk society. In a less demanding era, Socrates posed the situation as a learning paradox:

> *a person can learn only that which he doesn't know,*
> *but if he doesn't know it,*
> *how does he know what he is seeking to learn?*

I would like to take a few minutes to introduce some of the highlights of Transformation Theory (Mezirow, 1990, 1992), a theoretical model of how adults learn that I believe has particular relevance for adult education, for community development and for demystifying Socrates' learning paradox.

Transformation Theory suggests that we 'learn what we seek to learn' as the result of transforming our frame of reference. By redefining or reframing the problem we come to see our learning needs from a different perspective. This transformative learning occurs when we find that our old ways of understanding are no longer working well for us.

Transformation Theory is an explanation of how our **frames of reference** influence the way we make meaning and how they may be transformed to empower adult learners and to foster community development.

The Structure of Meaning

A frame of reference is the structure of assumptions with which we interpret our sense perceptions and, by doing so, create our experiences. Assumptions are taken-for-granted beliefs we have about reality. They often serve as tacit rules of thumb or are expressed as conventional wisdom that guides our actions. A culture is composed of shared frames of reference and these are acquired through cultural assimilation and are often reproduced through schooling.

Transformative learning experiences are emancipatory in that they free learners from the constraints and distortions of their own frames of reference. A more fully developed and dependable frame of reference is one that is more inclusive, differentiating, more open to alternative perspectives and more integrative of experience.

We learn in one of three ways: by *extending or refining* our existing frames of reference, by *learning new ones* or by *transforming* our existing frames of reference.

There are two dimensions to a frame of reference. One is our abstract **habits of expectation** – our 'meaning perspectives' that serve as filters or codes to shape, delimit and often distort our experience. Three sets of codes filter and constrain our understanding of reality: **socio-linguistic** (e.g. ideologies, norms, language codes), **psychological** (e.g. personality traits or repressed parental prohibitions that continue to dictate ways of feeling and acting in adulthood) and **epistemic** (e.g. learning styles, focusing on wholes vs. parts, on the concrete vs. the abstract, sensory preferences).

The second dimension of our frame of reference is the concrete result of our meaning perspective. This is our **point of view**, a 'meaning scheme' composed of the specific beliefs, feelings, judgments, intuitions and attitudes that accompany and shape a specific interpretation. For example, being ethnocentric (expecting groups other than your own to be inferior or threatening) is a generalized habit of expectation resulting in a point of view that is suspicious, demeaning, fearful or hostile toward a specific individual of a race, class, religion or nationality other than your own.

Transformative Learning

The process of transforming our frames of reference begins with critical reflection. What I mean by critical reflection is *the process of assessing one's assumptions and presuppositions*. Through critical reflection we can change the way we see the content of a problem or see our *process* of problem solving. This can result in transforming our meaning scheme or point of view. We may also become critically reflective of the *premises* upon which the problem is posed, how the problem is framed or defined. Premise reflection can lead to a transformation in our meaning perspective or habit of mind. It is easier to change our point of view because we can 'try on' a different point of view and see its relative advantage, but we cannot do this as easily with our habits of mind.

Let me give you an example of a perspective transformation from my own experience. For many years I worked in the field of community development in third world countries. I thought of my work as designed to provide new opportunities for village people to participate in decision making about their villages – to assign priorities (and provide the labour) for village improvement – building roads, drainage systems, schools, wells, health dispensaries, creating literacy and family planning programmes or adopting new agricultural methods. Governments or private organizations provided the technical assistance and materials necessary to complete the selected projects.

By their involvement in such projects, I believed villagers could learn a form of tutelary participatory democracy that would prepare them for subsequent full participation in political democracy. In this work, I would often focus critically on the ways of motivating villagers to participate in local projects – the *content* of my problem. I might also examine critically the *process* by which this model of community development could succeed – for example, could government officials, schooled in a rigid, colonial, civil service system, be rethreaded and succeed as community development agents? My point of view about my work changed significantly as I assessed my assumptions and acquired insight into each of these and other content and process questions.

In the 1970s, I encountered the writings of Paulo Freire and Ivan Illich and was jarred into an awareness that challenged the validity of my very premise regarding adult learning thorough participatory action in community development projects as preparation for active citizenship in political democracy. Freire pointed out a crucial missing dimension in my mental model: '*conscientization*' (critical reflection), the empowering learning process by which villagers change their traditional frames of reference by becoming aware and critical of their assumptions about their long established dependency relationships with those who controlled their lives – often the big landowner – *patrón* or *zamindar* – exploitive merchants, employers or political leaders – and take collective action on their reflective insights to effect social change.

Critical reflection on the limitations of my assumptions about adult education for community development transformed my taken-for-granted meaning perspective. I was forced to significantly modify a set of norms and roles that I had accepted without question determining the way I had thought of community development education (a socio-linguistic code that constituted a meaning perspective). My whole focus on how to work in adult education changed, my practice changed and my professional interests in research and adult learning theory were redirected, a process extending over the past two decades. In Freire's terms, I had an experience in conscientization; in the parlance of the womens' movement, I was engaged in consciousness raising, in psychotherapeutic terms, I achieved theoretical reflection – a metacognitive awareness of my own strategy for solving my problem. In the terminology of Transformation Theory, I experienced a perspective transformation.

Forms of Critical Reflection

There are different functions of critical reflection. One, 'objective reframing', may involve the critical review of a text or a pause in the instrumental action of problem solving to identify a new metaphor that redefines the problem. 'Action learning', as this concept is found in management training, brings together managers with diverse specializations and frames of reference to explore new ways to pose or solve a problem. The focus is on the objective problem rather than on oneself.

Another dimension, 'subjective reframing' pertains to critical *self*-reflection and involves examining the *reasons* why we have acquired distorted or dysfunctional frames of reference, their nature and their consequences. Subjective reframing involves critically examining the constitutive process of frame formation itself.

Subjective reframing is involved in the most significant transformative learning experiences. Subjective reframing is a common feature of adult learning and is exemplified by my own perspective transformation reported above. Various forms of educational intervention designed to foster subjective reframing include Freire's educational approach, consciousness raising groups, and cognitive psychotherapy.

Learning Domains

It is important to differentiate between two kinds of learning. One is **instrumental learning** – learning to control or manipulate the environment – task oriented learning with the purpose of improving performance. The other is learning what others mean when they communicate with us – **communicative learning** – that involves intentions, values, feelings and moral decisions. Both the learning process and appropriate educational interventions are very different for each.

In instrumental learning, what is communicated may be tested empirically through measurement to determine whether it is true, i.e. whether it is as it has been asserted to be. Reasoning involves making hypotheses and deductively testing them. In communicative learning, however, what is communicated does not often give itself to empirical tests of truth. Here we are concerned with the *justification* of an interpretation or a belief – we need to know not only whether it is true, but is it coherent, are feelings expressed authentic, is it appropriate to a given set of norms, is the person communicating truthful or attempting to deceive? Reasoning proceeds by identifying a metaphor and letting each step in exploring the implications of the analogy suggest the next one. As educators, our goal in communicative learning is to assist learners to negotiate their own meanings and values rather than to passively accept social reality as defined by others. This is what transformative learning is about.

Collaborative Discourse

There are only four ways to establish the validity or justification of a problematic belief or an interpretation – by turning to tradition, to authority, (the courts, politics or religion), to brute force, or by turning to discourse.

Unlike ordinary everyday discussion or dialogue, **collaborative discourse** involves an exclusive focus on the content – deliberately weighing the evidence, assessing arguments or reasons advanced in support or opposition, examining alternative viewpoints and on critically examining assumptions in order to reach a best judgment on the justification of a belief. An institutionalised model of collaborative discourse is the university seminar.

We turn for collaborative discourse to those we believe will be the most informed, 'objective' and rational to assess the justification of the interpretation we are making or our belief. We turn to those whom we trust, and discourse is more effective when participants share a sense of what Habermas calls *empathic solidarity*. The resulting consensual judgments are contingent; i.e. judgments that are useful until we encounter new and more persuasive perspectives, evidence or arguments that subsequent discourse establishes as yielding better judgments. This is a continuing process. We do not always agree, but through collaborative discourse, we can better understand or we may find a synthesis of opposing views.

The assumptions of rational discourse are that beliefs should contain no logical contradictions, reasons for believing them can be advanced and assessed, concepts will become more intelligible when analysed and we have criteria with which to know when the belief is justified or not.

The Conditions of Collaborative Discourse

Jürgen Habermas (1984) holds that the ideal conditions of undistorted rational discourse are implied in the very nature of human communication. However, if you are uncomfortable with the concept of universal ideals, as many post-modernists are, then certainly, this ideal of undistorted communication is implied in any democratic society or in any society that wishes to foster democracy. Ideally, the conditions of rational discourse are also ideal conditions of effective adult learning. As such, they are crucial to educational efforts to facilitate adult learning.

Participants must have:

- a feeling of trust and empathic solidarity with those participating in discourse;

- accurate and full information;

- freedom from coercion and distorting self-deception;

- equal opportunity to participate in discussion, to have their voices heard and understood.

Participants in an ideal adult discourse will also have previously learned to:

- weigh evidence and assess arguments objectively;

- respect alternative perspectives;

- critically reflect upon presuppositions and their consequences;

- accept an informed, objective, rational consensus as a legitimate test of validity of a belief, pending more evidence or argument.

Freedom, equality, participatory democracy, tolerance, solidarity, caring, inclusiveness are social values implicit in the ideal process of making meaning through collaborative discourse.

These values are rooted in the nature of human communication, rather than in the Western idealism of the Enlightenment. They also constitute a defining concept of community.

Of course, like every other ideal, ideal discourse seldom exists in our common experience. We all could point to the devastating distortions created by inequalities in the distribution of power and influence associated with race or ethnicity, gender, and class that distort one's ability to participate under such idealized circumstances. But as an ideal, this model of undistorted communication provides us with a goal and standard against which to judge our efforts as learners and as educators.

We can also use the ideal conditions of human discourse to judge our society's efforts or lack of efforts to foster these crucial conditions of learning. This is why adult educators become social activists. As learners in a democracy become aware of how taken-for-granted, oppressive, social norms and practices and institutionalised cultural ideologies have restrained or distorted their own beliefs, they become understandably motivated toward taking collective action to make social institutions and systems more responsive to the needs of those they serve. Whether, when and how they do so depends upon situational factors. Some react to critically achieved insights negatively by dropping out or seeking escape by immersion in alternative life styles or modes of dress.

Learning to participate openly, critically and empathically in collaborative discourse is crucial for adult learners. Learning to facilitate this kind of learning is indispensable for educators of adults. It is the particular function of adult educators to create communities of collaborative discourse in which distortions in communication due to differences in power and influence are minimized. Educators work with adult learners to deliberately create and enforce norms conducive to undistorted communication. Learning reflective participation in collaborative discourse and in social action is central to adult learning and to the development of learning communities.

Community Development

Adult educators concerned with community development encourage learners to become aware of community problems and to participate actively in collective community problem solving efforts. This involves two areas of practice. One involves fostering critical reflection on social conditions, practices, institutions, systems and traditional frames of reference that distort communication and constrain learning. In the context of families, educational institutions, organisations and in the broader community the adult educator's role is the same. It is to develop true communities of collaborative discourse leading to action. This will often involve providing protective learning environments and helping learners learn to discourse effectively.

The other community development function of adult educators is to help adult learners who have already become aware of the need for collective social action to learn what they need to know to act effectively. This often requires specialized knowledge and the services of an adult educator experienced in social action education.

Although adult educators do not become leaders, advocates or organizers of collective social action, they may help learners learn how to assume these roles, to anticipate and plan to overcome constraining situational factors, to deal with emotional resistance to taking action or to find relevant information needed to act.

The social context is of great importance in determining whether transformative learning will result in collective social action. For example, this is much more likely to happen when such learning occurs within the context of a social movement that involves serving a larger cause, many role models, group support, opportunities for collaborative discourse and encourages active participation in social action.

People interact in communities according to patterns of pre-set traditions, through efficient systems, which organize people along planned lines, and through the communicative exchange of reasons leading to agreement among them. Adult education is about helping people learn to coordinate their actions openly to reach understandings. For adult educators, community development means fostering learning communities in which people can reflect critically, discourse collaboratively and act collectively.

Transformation theory envisions an ideal society composed of communities of learners engaged in a continuing collaborative inquiry to determine the truth or arrive at a tentative best judgment about alternative beliefs, a community cemented by empathic solidarity, committed to the social and political practice of participatory democracy, informed through critical reflection, continuously engaged in collaborative discourse and collectively taking reflective action, when necessary, to assure that social systems and local institutions, organizations, and practices are responsive to the human needs of those they serve.

References

Habermas, J. (1988). *The theory of communicative action. Vol I. Reason and the rationalization of society* (T. McCarthy, Trans.). Boston: Beacon Press.

Mezirow, J. (1991). *Transformative dimensions of adult learning.* Oxford: Jossey-Bass.

Mezirow, J. & Associates. (1990). *Fostering critical reflection in adulthood.* Oxford: Jossey-Bass.

Update on
Transformative Learning

JACK MEZIROW
COLUMBIA UNIVERSITY

Update on Transformative Learning

JACK MEZIROW
COLUMBIA UNIVERSITY

Transformative learning has evolved in the United States and is a generally accepted but still contentious theory in adult education. There have been six international conferences on this subject in North America, involving over 300 presentation papers, the publication of over a dozen books, more than 50 doctoral dissertations and the creation of a professional journal, *Journal of Transformative Education*.

Transformative learning refers to the process by which we transform problematic frames of reference (mind sets, meaning perspectives) – sets of assumptions and expectation – to make them more inclusive, discriminating, open, reflective and emotionally able to change. Such frames are better because they are more likely to generate beliefs and opinions that will prove more true or justified to guide action.

Frames of reference include the:

- *sociolinguisic* – involving cultural canon, social norms, customs, ideologies, paradigms, linguistic frames, language games, political orientations, occupational and organizational cultures, habits of mind;

- *moral/ethical* – involving conscience and moral norms and values;

- *learning styles* – sensory preferences, focus on wholes or parts or on the concrete or abstract, and working alone or together;

- *religious* – commitment to doctrine, spiritual or transcendental world views;

- *psychological* – theories, schemas, scripts, self-concept, personality traits or types, repressed parental prohibitions, emotional response patterns and dispositions;

- *health* – ways of interpreting health problems, rehabilitation, near death experience;

- *aesthetic* – values, taste, attitude, standards, judgments about beauty and the insight and authenticity of aesthetic expressions.

The doctoral programme, AEGIS – Adult Education Guided Independent Study – a highly selective doctoral programme that I established at Teachers College, Columbia University, to study transformative learning – has recently celebrated its 20th anniversary. In its original form, carefully selected applicants with at least five years significant professional experience in adult education were admitted to the programme. Students came on campus one weekend a month and attended intensive three-week summer sessions to satisfy EdD course requirements in two years. Dialogue continued in this period through the internet. AEGIS has attracted students commuting to monthly classes from as far away as Alaska and Saudi Arabia.

Applicants were required to select a contested problem in adult education and to write a paper identifying opposing viewpoints, indicating their own position. They were also instructed to write an analysis of taken-for-granted assumptions implicit in their viewpoint. The paper was returned with a detailed analysis of missing assumptions, often involving several pages, with a request the applicant rewrite with a focus on their own assumptions. The rewrite was also often returned pointing out limitations in their rewrite of assumptions.

This exercise was designed to challenge taken-for-granted ways of thinking. Even among leaders in adult education, the concept of assumption analysis, especially involving epistemic assumptions, was not fully recognized as a significant dimension of adult learning (Kitchener & King, 1990).

Courses in AEGIS included Assumption Analysis, in which groups of six analysed assumptions of authors of the literature of adult education, Life History, in which individuals in groups of three each examined the life decisions that led them to come together in this experimental adult education programme. Participants gained insight from an examination of how significant life decisions were often made and predicated on differing and unquestioned assumptions.

Courses included Ideology, the work of Paulo Freire, interpreting popular media, art and applications in adult education – all from the perspective of transformative learning. The programme has been adapted over the years to reflect changing perspectives and priorities of students and new faculty.

The original research base for the concept of transformative learning evolved from a comprehensive national study of women returning to re-entry programmes in community colleges in the United States at the height of the women's movement which saw an unprecedented attendance of women in higher education (Mezirow, 1978).

The study used grounded theory research methodology to conduct intensive field studies of students in 12 diverse college programmes, a comprehensive analytical description of an additional 24 programmes and responses to a mail enquiry involving another 314.

In this study transformations often followed the following phases of meaning becoming clarified:

(1)   a disorienting dilemma;

(2)   self examination with feelings of fear, anger, guilt or shame;

(3)   a critical assessment of assumptions;

(4)   recognition that one's discontent and the process of transformation are shared;

(5)   exploration of options for new roles, relationships and action;

(6)   planning a course of action;

(7)   acquiring knowledge and skills for implementing one's role;

(8)   provisional trying of new roles;

(9)   building competence and self confidence in new roles and relationships;

(10)   a reintegration into one's life on the basis of conditions dictated by one's new perspective.

Transformations may be epochal – a sudden major reorientation in habit of mind, often associated with significant life crises, or a cumulative progressive sequence of insights resulting in changes in point of view and leading to a transformation in habit of mind.

My interpretation of transformative learning has been challenged by several colleagues for my emphasis placed on reasoning and epistemology in analysing transformative learning, what they believe to be my neglect of important emotional and spiritual dimensions, and my failure to recognize what they believe should be the primacy of ideology, power and the goal of social action in interpreting the nature of adult learning.

Transformative learning, as I understand it, suggests that conscience, awareness, control of one's thoughts and the transformation of meaning structures are central to the adult learning process and to adult education.

Transformative learning is an adult dimension of reason assessment involving the validation and reformulation of meaning structures. For adult education, this theory suggests the centrality of the process of critical reflection on epistemic assumptions.

Epistemic assumptions refer to critically assessing the source, constitution, relevance, consequences and appropriateness of reasons supporting assumptions.

The process of transformative learning involves:

■   reflecting critically on the source, nature, and consequences of relevant assumptions, our own and those of others;

- assessing instrumental learning – learning involved in controlling and manipulating the environment, in improving performance and prediction – by empirically testing contested beliefs about the truth of an assertion;

- assessing communicative learning – the meaning of what is being communicated – by arriving at a tentative, more justified belief, by participating freely and fully in an informed continuing discourse;

- taking action on our transformed perspective – we make a decision and live what we have come to believe until we encounter new evidence, argument or a perspective that renders our orientation problematic and requires reassessment;

- acquiring a disposition – to become more critically reflective of our own assumptions and those of others, to seek validation of our transformative insights through further empirical research or through more freely and fully participating in discourse and to follow through on our decision to act upon a transformed insight.

References

Kitchener, K. & King, P. (1990). The reflective judgment model. In J. Mezirow & Associates, *Fostering critical reflection in adulthood.* San Francisco: Jossey-Bass.

Mezirow, J. (1975). *Education for perspective transformation: Women's re-entry programs in Community Colleges.* New York: Center for Adult Education, Teachers College, Columbia University.

'Really Useful Knowledge': Linking Theory and Practice

JANE THOMPSON
PRINCIPAL RESEARCH OFFICER
NIACE

'Really Useful Knowledge': Linking Theory and Practice

JANE THOMPSON
PRINCIPAL RESEARCH OFFICER
NIACE

In the run up to the forthcoming American Presidential elections a bemused British journalist Charles Wheeler asks one of Bob Dole's closest advisers 'Why has it taken Bob Dole so long to get round to telling us about his principles and about the kinds of concerns he feels deeply about? We've had no sense so far of a man who is informed or guided by anything other than the 'immediate' (*Newsnight*, August 16, 1996). The adviser replies that Dole is 'a doer' so busy with the 'mechanics of politics' the day-to-day demands of 'getting things done.' Being responsible for the 'mechanics' and 'getting things done' means you don't have a lot of time (apparently) to think very much about the greater scheme of things, why you make some choices rather than others, where your actions fit, what might be the consequences of what you do. We are meant to be impressed by a 'practical man' who rolls up his shirtsleeves and who is quick off the mark when it comes to getting things done. John Major has been quick off the mark in cultivating the same approach as he takes off his jacket, rolls up his sleeves, climbs onto his soap box and sets about answering prearranged questions from a carefully invited audience most recently from the stage of the Tory party conference in Bournemouth (October, 1996) A strategy supposed to indicate practical politics, the common touch. 'Did you like it?' He grins enthusiastically. Desperately trying to reinforce the presentation of himself as 'Honest John the boy from Brixton' who does what's best for Britain without getting too tied up by philosophy or ideology. Unlike Tony Blair who is still associated in many people's minds inaccurately as it happens with ideas that derive from socialism.

In the case of Dole the existence of any grander narrative is denied almost as a testimony to action rather than theory. Probably it's not so surprising. Politics on both sides of the Atlantic in recent years have been characterised by short termism and pragmatism; revealing the cynicism of bland faced re definitions of the latest U-turn enforced resignation or scandal whilst skilfully avoiding the principled point; responding to what is immediate and leaving the medium or long term future to take care of itself. Or to someone else to sort out. Especially in relation to the environment. Short term thinking in Britain currently finds the Tories embarrassingly keen to sell off and get rid of anything and everything which still remains within the public sector, before an in coming Labour Government can get their hands on it including British Rail, the administration of the Social Security system, Ministry of Defence housing, and the Post Office. Whilst the Labour Party is busily shedding its philosophic commitment to historic left of centre principles for fear of being considered too dangerous, too visionary, too radical or too socialist by those whose votes they want to count on.

On both sides of the Atlantic the struggle for political power is being contested by individuals who seem to grow increasingly similar to each other (in terms of ethnicity, class, gender and ideas), with similar allegiances to corporate interests, and who seem more and more concerned to represent only those groups who have the same kind of stake as themselves in what is currently defined as society. Leaving the ones who are left 'the rest' and 'the others' more and more excluded. In the US this means that on a good day almost half the population will not exercise their vote in presidential elections and more than half won't bother to vote in congressional and senate elections. (That's if they're even registered.) Not because they are apathetic or disillusioned or stupid. But because the circumstances of their existence has little or no bearing on the agenda of either of the two presidential candidates and does not feature within the priorities of either of the two main parties which govern the United States. Why should urban ghetto dwellers, without jobs and without welfare, or Native Americans whose lands have been plundered, or Mexican immigrants who are denied citizenship rights, or rural black cotton pickers, housed in shacks along the muddy flatlands of the Mississippi go through the motions of voting for individuals and parties that have little knowledge of their lives, and even less interest in finding out, except to keep them in check? Why would they be persuaded that their vote might 'make a difference' when they have no evidence to support the accuracy of such an obvious piece of ideology? In such circumstances, despite the platitudes and rhetoric about democracy, the widespread non-participation in voting by groups who have been effectively disenfranchised is not actually seen as a major cause for concern by those whose interests are reflected in the political system. Not voting is a consequence, and has by now become a necessary characteristic, of what counts as democracy, and which sustains the particular brand of un representation established as a political system in the United States.

In Britain the trends are similar though not yet so extreme. Seventeen years of right wing Conservative governments have deepened the divisions between rich and poor; between those living in 'traditional families' and those who do not; between those who have jobs and roofs over their heads and those who do not; between those who are white and those who are black. Probably also between those who are young and male, who are educated in run down schools lacking adequate resources, who are the ready targets for drugs and unfulfilled consumer aspirations, who have few prospects of either getting a job or buying into the housing market and those who are female or older, living in the same neighbourhoods, whose communities are being destroyed by the pressures of poverty, unemployment, hopelessness and increasing competition for scarce resources. These are divisions which in turn cement distinctions between those who do and who don't see any purpose in getting too excited about politics. For people without much recognisable power there is no obvious connection between putting a cross on a ballot paper and changing their experience of society. In Margaret Thatcher's immortal words there is no such thing as 'society' and by definition less and less reason to assume any responsibility for anyone other than oneself. Whether one has power or not. Hers is something of a non-society, in which minorities who live in poverty, like single parents (mostly women), the elderly (mostly women), young unemployed, people with the kind of disabilities which prevent them from working and in some cases from looking after themselves, as well as different ethnic minorities (who can be found in all the other categories as well) are termed by some an 'under class' and by others 'scroungers.' Whatever the label, these are groups of people who have less and less reason to vote in conventional elections for politicians whose world view is increasingly shaped by the assumption that democracy is about representation rather than participation, that charters can guarantee citizens rights, that legislation concerned with the protection of welfare provision, workers rights, environmental sanity, and even human rights, must always, it seems, be subject to restrictions on public spending, the promotion of free market competition and the maintenance of a strong and centralised state committed to defending corporate profits.

In such circumstances politicians like Dole and Clinton in the United States do not need to articulate the theories which inform their policies. They are implicit. Their actions speak for themselves and have been understood as such by all of those who take no interest in elections. That's why they've voted with their feet. In Britain, and in other advanced industrialised societies for all I know, which are similarly committed to free market economics and restrictions on public spending, the slide towards political systems which operate on the basis of widespread non-participation, especially by those who have little stake in what is on offer, is a 'price worth paying' according to those whose social and economic advantage is secured by such arrangements. In these circumstances, minority groups of numerous kinds, with little purchase on power, and few advocates in high places, are easy enough to stereotype and to hold responsible for their own alleged deficiencies. It is commonplace, for example, according to dominant definitions of social reality, to account for the continuing inequalities between men and women, including increased levels of male violence and child sexual abuse, as being the choice of women who are 'their own worst enemies' or else the fault of nasty feminists who wear the 'wrong kind of clothes' and can't 'agree among themselves' about what should be done. It is assumed that the widespread demoralisation of entire communities by unemployment, cuts in public spending, poor health born of poverty, restrictive legislation and the intensification of punitive policing policies, is in fact the result of apathy, welfare dependency, a general decline in morality, poor parenting skills and the absence of any sense of personal responsibility. In such communities increasing numbers of people don't vote and don't readily participate in the processes of decision making which affect their lives. And whilst conventional wisdom denounces them for their fecklessness and pathological deficiencies, the gulf between those who do have recognisable interests to defend, and those whose material conditions are barely taken seriously, continues to widen.

Meanwhile political recourse to pragmatism, dignified as some kind of virtue which is said to 'get things done', disguises the extent to which underlying, profound and quite self conscious theoretic principles have actually determined the character of what is taking shape.

Those who are concerned about education will have noticed the same pre occupation in recent years with 'getting things done' rather than 'wasting time' on theories and debating philosophy students into courses, throughput, output, progression routes, research profiles, accreditation schemes, calculations of competence, quality assurance, performance indicators, league tables, the appointment of management consultants, the development of marketing strategies, the measurement of everything that moves on a five point scale all turned into statistics and graphs designed to produce efficiency savings and to release money from government funding agencies. At the same time education is being transformed into training. Judgements regarding excellence are increasingly determined on behalf of employers, and measured by inspectors employed by government appointed quangos, who are required to stimulate competition and to establish financial targets built upon systems of penalties. Academics have become managers. Managers need have no previous 'hands on *experience'* of education. Students and adult learners are spoken of as consumers. Teachers are regarded as potential revolutionaries and/or incompetents, who need to be motivated by the threat of losing their jobs, and monitored by excessive amounts of bureaucracy, as a way of using up their energy and distracting them from exercising too much critical intelligence. Like their teachers, students and learners are generally required to think as little as possible, to question even less, and to concentrate on accumulating credits and developing competencies which can be assessed by forms that can be measured by machines. As more and more people collect credits (rather like lottery tickets) which lead to qualifications that are widely considered to be totally unconnected to mind expanding or life transforming *experience* not to mention having little or no relationship to interesting, useful or well paid employment (if at all) it would now seem a matter of real urgency to consider what all of this might signify. Especially if one retains some illusions about participation being a necessary ingredient of democracy. And some conviction that education can also be a weapon in the war against poverty. A weapon which might indeed be used to overcome discrimination, exploitation, exclusion and violence. Which can assist in the process of transforming societies based on inequalities, vested interests and injustice into societies in which all citizens are more directly involved in the decision making which shapes their lives. Not simply as individuals who, in the spirit of free enterprise and self reliance, have personal responsibilities and duties to perform, and who become locked into competition for scarce resources which are frequently secured at the expense of others. But as members of collectivities which share material and social conditions that derive from the recognition of interdependence and mutual regard. And which are based on the simple conviction that no one is truly free until we all are. A conviction grounded in shared social and communal responsibilities, and the expectation of generalised participation in decision-making, however local. Which is guided by a vision that extends beyond the boundaries of what is to what *might* be and to the kind of understandings which take account of wider, international and global considerations.

You may by now be wondering what all this has got to do with 'really useful knowledge' and 'linking theory and practice.' Social and political systems which create exclusion and lack of participation in decision making seriously damage peoples lives. People don't on the whole get angry. Creative anger could be constructive. They get demoralised or disaffected. We might like to think that communities in crisis automatically develop a wonderful 'sense of togetherness' and 'community spirit' which 'keeps them going' despite the odds. But they are just as likely more likely perhaps to release feelings of frustration and alienation upon each other rather than on the structural and political causes of their hopelessness. Men living in communities which are in crisis initiate more criminal activity at the expense of each other, more domestic violence, more racist attacks. Their communities are the breeding grounds for anti democratic and extremist responses to the accumulation of grievances born of economic depression and lack of recognition. These are not the kind of responses which education can resolve. But they are the kind of circumstances in which 'particular kinds of education' might have a part to play. And by this I don't mean league tables and quality assurance mechanisms. Or aromatherapy for beginners. I mean political education.

In adult education there is a long tradition, dating back to at least the nineteenth century, even longer if we include the writing of Mary Wolstonecraft, concerned with the relationship between education and social change. The radical tradition in adult education has argued not simply for knowledge which is deemed to be 'the best that has been thought and said' which is the basis of the extra mural and liberal traditions. Or for knowledge that is vocational and practical in order to make people into more skilful and responsible workers which is the antecedent of the current pre occupation with training. Or for knowledge which is devoid of any social context but is related to 'personhood' and 'individual self fulfilment' the concern of the essentially American 'human growth' school of thinking popular in the seventies. The radical tradition in adult education judges 'the usefulness' of knowledge in relation to its contribution to assisting social and political change. Especially in relation to those whose social, material and political conditions are based on oppression, inequality or exploitation. All words which are fairly unfashionable in these days of postmodern, free market and entrepreneurial thinking. But not I think obsolete as lived conditions. When chartists and Christian socialists and co operators and feminists and early trade union organisers argued for working class and women's education in the nineteenth century they wanted 'really useful knowledge' that would help them to understand both the nature of their present condition and how to get out of it. 'Really useful knowledge' was political knowledge which could be used to challenge the relations of oppression and inequality from which they suffered. In this sense arguments about the liberationary possibilities of education have a long history within the agendas of progressive political movements concerned with overcoming structural injustices and inequalities.

The radical tradition in adult education based on 'really useful knowledge' implies the development of critical thinking, the recognition of human agency, political growth and the confidence to challenge what is generally taken for granted as inevitable. It means deriving theory from the authority of lived material experience, and using it in ways which connect with the similar or related experiences of others, in order to establish a 'critical mass' which can join together to develop collective forms of social action to achieve political change. The emphasis is not on 'competitive individualism' or the pursuit of 'individual rights' at the expense of others. But on communal responses to confronting related oppressions and to promoting change. Its about another old fashioned word the significance of praxis, of relating theory to practice, in which one informs the other, in a continuing and dialectical process of making changes on the basis of applying critical intelligence to what is understood from experience in ways that re constitute both the situation and the subject.

Deriving theory from experience and in turn relating it to practice is far from being a crude mechanical or behaviourist approach. It allows for the exploration of 'meaning' and of how people make sense of their lived experiences. It allows for comparisons to be made with the meanings articulated by others. It can connect the understanding of individuals and collectivities of individuals in ways that create a critical mass. It also has something useful to contribute to the understanding of what constitutes power. Power does not lie simply in the remit of dominant groups who download it so to speak onto less powerful victims. It does operate in this way, and structural supports for the accumulation and administration of power are clearly the backdrop against which any opportunities for the redistribution of power, the renegotiation of power based relationships, and the recognition of available room in which to manoeuvre, must be measured. But the exercise of power, and what might be re defined as power, is also present within all of us, and within the relationships we make with each other. To be exercised in more or less oppressive or more or less egalitarian ways. Focused with energy and precision, and informed by the determination 'to get out from under' the power within us can be released in the service of liberation just as possibly as it can be constrained by feelings of despair or alienation.

Social changes are not simply determined by structural conditions. Or by significant individuals with superior qualities of leadership or charisma or ruthlessness. The history of social movements is a history of people operating in the cracks of superstructures. Of using the energies generated at the margins of systems and organisations. Of exercising considerable imagination, critical thinking, subversion and undutiful behaviour to destabilise and de construct the authority of the inevitable. All of them ways of 'taking back control' based on the inter relationship between consciousness and courage, between theory and practice. Taking back control and joining with others in collective action to achieve change is at the root of concepts like participation and democracy. It finds its impetus in human agency and can transform people's lives. As well as transforming views about oneself.

All of which might sound enormously idealistic and highly abstract. But anyone who has experienced what it feels like to say No to different forms of oppression, or to engage creatively and seriously with others in a piece of social action concerned to get something established or something changed which more powerful interests have determined must continue, will know how contagious the release of human possibility can be. Even in defeat there is the further possibility of making progress, so long as the expectation of having collective rights to participation and exercising some control over one's material conditions are allowed to enter the collective consciousness. This is precisely what Freire has discussed as conscientization in relation to education as the practice of freedom. (Freire, 1972) It's what bell hooks refers to as 'transgression' in which the academy, the classroom, the neighbourhood drop in centre anywhere in which learning is taking place may not be paradise, but is a place where paradise can be created. With all its limitations (the classroom/the neighbourhood/the drop in centre) remains a location of possibility (where we can) collectively go beyond boundaries, to 'transgress.' According to bell hooks, this is also education as the 'practice of freedom' (hooks, 1994, p. 207).

And just in case you imagine that the pursuit of social change from below, based on conscientization, the development of critical intelligence and the courage to be undutiful in the interests of transgression, all implies a form of 'really useful knowledge' which is only related to the disciplines of politics, economics and social science, I would remind you of what the late great Audre Lorde had to say about making new knowledge and about developing our own ways of doing things. Even she might have stopped short at the prospect of 'aromatherapy for beginners' being regarded as having any political or emancipatory significance but she would have encouraged us to make use of every available opportunity to connect popular education to the self conscious struggle for popular liberation from oppressions. She was not talking simply about access and required us to remember that 'the masters tools will never dismantle the masters house' (Lorde, 1981, p. 98). In other words, that access to wider powers without some transformation of the systems of power will not be sufficient to deliver the kinds of changes we might envision.

Thinking beyond conventional forms of wisdom and the alleged logic of present systems is a further variation on the theme of 'really useful knowledge' and is connected to what another black poet, June Jordan, has to say in relation to the importance of poetry, political consciousness and language. She says, good poetry and successful revolutions change our lives. (But) you cannot compose a good poem or wage a revolution without changing consciousness. And you cannot alter consciousness unless you 'attack the language that you share with your enemies and invent a language that you share with your allies' (Jordan, 1994, pp. 70 1). Part of the residual problem with liberal as distinct from radical approaches to the dilemmas posed by education for social change is the widespread assumption that what you need to do is 'modify your language' (and your appearance and your dress code) to lull potential power holders into a false sense of security about your reasonableness and moderation. Even to change your language, so that it is 'less confrontational', i.e. less associated with 'unpopular' world views like feminism, socialism or Marxism. The problem with calling Women's rights 'gender studies', or lesbianism 'sexual preference', or anti discrimination 'equal opportunities', or unemployment 'flexibility', or redundancy 'efficiency savings', or privatisation 'consumer choice', or education 'training', or democratic rights 'customer contracts' or 'client's charters', however, is that the modification of the language changes its meaning and its impact. It also means that you quickly forget the point at which you began to adopt the language of the enemy as a strategy to gain acceptance, with the intention of 'working from within.' It soon becomes 'second nature' to you, and the repertoire with which you then make sense of the world. Except that you are likely to be making sense of the world in a significantly altered way, as you become progressively wedded to the concepts and concerns of those whose interests might be very different to your own, and into which you have now become incorporated. 'Really useful knowledge' in this sense implies vigilance, imagination, courage and taking trouble to be free.

The ideas related to the notion of 'really useful knowledge' also offers us a way of thinking about adult education now, as a form of popular education for democracy, and in relation to debates about active citizenship and more widespread participation in decision making. Debates which might have relevance at a local level to inform social action campaigns; in political movements of various kinds; as antidotes to the widespread domination of public life by white, middle class, able bodied men but also to address the responsibilities implied in the protection of human rights, environmentalism and globalisation. In this sense I would recommend you to take a look at the report recently produced by the Women and Citizenship Research Group in association with the Equal Opportunities Commission for Northern Ireland (1995) called *Women and citizenship: Power, participation and choice* (EOC, 1995).

The research starts with the reluctance of women to say they engage in politics, or at least Politics with a capital P, a reluctance which is widespread across Europe. Reluctance should not be read as ignorance or apathy however. It partly stems from constitutional arrangements and partly from historic – and patriarchal mechanisms of exclusion. It partly implies a definition of what constitutes politics and which doesn't take account of, for example, community activism, campaigning, membership of voluntary organisations and pressure groups or social movements. It also stems from the ways in which power is mediated within communities by additional considerations of gender, age, ethnicity and the like. Frequently, women have been required to subsume their interests as women to other loyalties which might be defined by others as 'more important.'

Citizenship is, by the way, one of those buzz words which can mean very different things to different people and needs to be used with caution. The Tory government in Britain uses citizenship to preach ideologies of self help and self reliance and is intended to promote personal contributions to the common good. According to modern Conservatism, citizens' rights are seen as being analogous to consumers' rights, in ways that can be underwritten by public charters. Except that patients charters have done very little to guarantee an effective health system which responds quickly and appropriately when people are sick. Travellers' charters don't make the trains run on time, or increase safety standards undermined by de regulation, or address the imminent collapse of the transport infrastructure. Consumers' charters haven't prevented fat cats from making enormous profits out of privatising public utilities or persuaded them to make personal contributions to the common good. Individualised complaints procedures, administered by quangos, don't compensate for taking power away from democratically elected local authorities or restricting trade union activities. Definitions of citizenship which require people to behave themselves and do what the state wants are not good reasons in themselves for promoting active citizenship.

The same problems emerge in adopting an uncritical enthusiasm for an 'individual rights' mentality. In Britain the pressure group Liberty (once the Council for Civil Liberties) retains an essentially liberal and libertarian attitude to protecting peoples rights, and is based on a philosophy of liberalism which has got a lot more in common with Thatcherism than many people would like to imagine. Personally I cannot accept that an individual's right to participate in the production and dissemination of child pornography, for example, can simply be viewed as a matter of personal conscience or choice. Or that it's unfair to arrest sex tourists in Britain on the basis of what they get up to in the Philippines and Thailand. Discussions about rights which are expressed only in individual terms, or in relation to the concerns of specific groups, don't get us very far along the road when it comes to challenging structural oppressions like racism, imperialism and sexism.

The concerns of the Women and Citizenship Research project are somewhat more modest. But extremely important. The main focus of the research is about the long exclusion of women from the sphere of legal and political rights, and from active participation in decision making bodies in the public sphere. A secondary focus deals with what might be the significance of women's greater inclusion. The report notes the absence of women in public life in Northern Ireland compared to men, and compared to the situation in Great Britain, which is in itself not very inspiring. The writers also consider the Republic of Ireland in which some changes for the better have occurred during the last twenty years. Most notably the election of Mary Robinson as President and increasing numbers of women in the Dáil – 12 per cent in 1994 as against 7.8 per cent in 1989. (As in Britain still some way to go, I would say). In discussing some of these concerns with women's groups of various kinds the report is able to make a number of recommendations which would give women more influence and more representation. These involve recommendations directed towards Womens organisations, towards political parties and politicians, and towards policy makers in the voluntary and statutory sectors. It is interesting to note the extent to which the recommendations deal with issues about power. And so far as the contribution made by education is concerned, how important it is seen to be to develop content that is related to raising political, economic and feminist awareness, as well as developing the kinds of skills which can turn heightened awareness into effective practice. The main education recommendation, in fact, is to promote political education, based on what I would call 'really useful knowledge', with a view to increasing the direct participation of women in decision making and public life. In practice this would mean transforming the culture of existing political institutions and decision making bodies not simply to make them more women friendly and reflective of Womens issues, but in order to reconstitute some of the assumptions about what counts as political concerns from a women's point of view. This would provoke many more debates and in turn policies about environmental issues, community concerns, child care, women's employment rights, reproductive and health rights, and issues concerning violence against women, for example, than is currently on the agendas of most malestream political parties. People in the audience will have their own ideas about what else a more gender balanced agenda might include.

This then is just one example. The work packs currently being produced by the Popular Education for Democracy Project at the Department of Continuing Education in Leeds is another. Neither is a blueprint. Different circumstances and different cultural contexts require different responses no doubt. Except the underlying principle remains the same. As adult educators, community development workers, volunteers and community activists we are all cultural workers whose energies and services can be called upon, as particular kinds of resources, to be used in the interests (or as inhibitors) of political change. We are likely to have no greater insight into what might constitute emancipatory learning than people whose communities, and whose life very often, depends upon it. Certainly our role is not to direct or control the energies which are released although we might want to lend solidarity and recognise commonalties where appropriate. Or express dissent. Certainly we all have significant oppressions of our own to be dealing with before we start thinking we can tell others what to do. But we ought to know about creating the kinds of learning spaces, and providing the kinds of content and learning opportunities, which enable groups of people facing oppressions and discrimination to identify what would be 'really useful knowledge' for them, in order to better understand their situations and to take action in pursuit of change. To turn theory into practice. As all of us in this room must also do.

Disclaiming theory in the pursuit of practicalities and 'rolling up the sleeves' to 'get things done' is a form of action without reflection. It sustains systems of oppression rather than acknowledging the complexities of how power and ideologies operate. It doesn't, in the end, do anyone we care about any favours. It's also bad faith.

Which brings me back to the point with which I began. Just because Bob Dole and Tony Blair and John Major are playing coy about the theories which inform their actions, it doesn't mean to say they haven't got any. They would be more honest and in the end, be held in higher regard by those they want to persuade – if they took the trouble to acknowledge them.

References

Freire, P. (1972). *Pedagogy of the oppressed.* London: Penguin.

hooks, bell, (1994). *Teaching to transgress: Education and the practice of freedom.* London: Routledge.

Jordan, J. (1994, March/April). Who's rocking the boat? *Ms Magazine.*

Lorde, A. (1981). In Moraga & Anzaldua (Eds.), *This bridge called my back: Writings by radical women of color.* Pittsburgh, PA: Persephone Press.

Popular Education for Democracy Project, Dept of Continuing Education, University of Leeds. Women and Citizenship Research Group. (1995). *Women and citizenship: Power, participation and choice.* Belfast: Equal Opportunities Commission for Northern Ireland.

The Road to Hell...

JANE THOMPSON
PRINCIPAL RESEARCH OFFICER
NIACE

The Road to Hell…

JANE THOMPSON
PRINCIPAL RESEARCH OFFICER
NIACE

Two years ago I was in Edinburgh for the Make Poverty History protest at the G8 summit in July. The grey haired woman on the bus from the National Pensioners' Convention was carrying a peace flag and wearing a Greenpeace t-shirt. Her rucksack was scattered with badges supporting the Anti-War Coalition and the Campaign for Nuclear Disarmament. Around her arm she wore white and red wristbands wanting to make capitalism, as well as poverty, history[1]. She was bending the ear of the young man sitting next to her: 'Why do politicians suddenly become stupid once they get elected? It always happens. This lot are the worst. Forget about making a ring around the city, I'd put a ring around their necks!'

You could see him trying to escape her onslaught, until she finally pushed the right button. 'How many hours a week do you work?' 'I can't get a job', the young man said. 'I come from Sudan. I want to work here but your government wants to send me home.' This was a public service bus, taking tourists to the Royal Mile and locals into town. Not one of the hundreds of charter buses carrying thousands of protesters from every corner of Britain to Edinburgh for the biggest demonstration in Scotland's history. The asylum seeker from Sudan got off the bus with the grey haired woman and they joined the march together.

You could tell that incidents and episodes like this were taking shape all over the place. The thing about a mass demonstration, with an urgent and progressive design, is that it is bigger than the self-interests of the individuals involved. It brings together lots of people from different walks of life, emboldened by the occasion and inspired by their mutual commitment, in the celebration of common purpose. For every one that actually joined the march in Edinburgh, there were a dozen others from their various supporters groups and networks back home, cheering them on.

Planning for the demonstration had begun six months earlier by the North South coalition of non-governmental organisations (NGOs), social movements, community based organisations (CBOs), charities, churches, pressure groups and social justice campaigns that make up the Global Call to Action Against Poverty (GCAP). Similar public demonstrations were taking place across Britain and the wider world as G8 leaders made

---

1   Make Poverty History is one of the larger campaigns associated with the Global Call to Action Against Poverty. Its symbol is a white wristband. Make Capitalism History is a campaigning slogan of the Scottish Socialist Party. Its symbol is a red wristband.

their way to Gleneagles in Scotland for a meeting in which world poverty and climate change were, for the first time, top of the agenda. In seventy-two countries, from Korea to Kenya and Australia to Peru, people dressed in white gathered in the streets, wearing white wristbands and demanding the elimination of extreme poverty (Naidoo 2005).

By the time the G8 leaders met together in Edinburgh, 10 million Britons had signed up to the Make Poverty History Campaign. One sixth of the British population knew that during the four days of deliberations in Scotland, 120,000 children in Africa alone would die because of poverty. Television companies had cleared their schedules to report in detail what would transpire. An entertaining, and not unproblematic, alliance between political activists and celebrities lent their energy and glamour to the occasion. Some gave the mistaken impression that the whole thing was invented and made possible because of the insistence and persistence of Bob Geldof.

But the sheer breadth and energy of this kind of engagement was already well established before the media made it fashionable. According to the World Development Movement, European and North American protests and pop concerts

were only one element of a much larger movement rooted in developing countries – showing that the fiercest critics of the International Monetary Fund (IMF) and World Bank policies were the people most affected by them.

(Mayo, 2005)

Reflecting on its millennium campaign to cancel third world debt, Jubilee 2000 argued that 'the world will never be the same again' as a result of huge numbers of people from civil society movements in both North and South mobilising to challenge the negative effects of globalisation, through citizen action, in solidarity beyond the nation state, to transform global agendas (Jubilee 2000 Coalition). Through the activities of NGOs, CBOs, social movements, issue campaigns and policy advocacy, citizens have been increasingly finding ways to make their voices heard and to influence the decisions and practices of larger institutions that affect their lives – both locally and globally (Thompson, 2005).

In the event, one of the most effective mobilisations of recent times, rooted in the struggles of those with least power and security in the world community, was denied its moment of absolute attention on the world stage. The detonating of four terrorist bombs in London, timed to coincide with the opening of the Summit at Gleneagles, shifted attention dramatically to a rather different kind of protest, which was equally well planned. As we should know, actions that spring from civil society associations and from 'the set of relational networks – formed for the sake of the family, faith, interests and ideology' do not necessarily lead to similar conclusions (Waltzer, 1992).

But even without the bombings, it was never likely that the G8 leaders would fulfil the hopes and commitments demanded by GCAP. Despite all the populist hype in the media – about the one room and the eight men with the capacity to make history – activists knew that the real decisions were being made elsewhere. They knew that some – but not much – debt would be cancelled. They knew that an announcement was to be made that would exaggerate an increase in aid. They knew there was to be some warm words about the importance of education and the fight against HIV/AIDs and malaria. Without the mass mobilisation, there would have been none of this. It is unlikely that poverty and climate change would have even been on the agenda.

But activists also knew that nothing deriving from the deliberations in Gleneagles would stem the lucrative flow of arms from the G8 to Africa and beyond. That no-one would do anything to save the three and a half million people currently starving in Niger. That no-one wanted to take a stand over Darfur. That discussions about trade tariffs would be shelved until the World Trade Organisation (WTO) meeting in December. That the decision to stand shoulder to shoulder with George Bush would require those holding more enlightened views on climate change to remain silent. And that when everyone went home, the back-tracking would begin. Those involved in GCAP were already planning what to do next to keep up the pressure.

Because of the London bombings, however, attention shifted back to the war on terror. The G8 leaders were able to slip away without much adverse comment on how little they had conceded to the poor or to the planet. George Bush was able to return to the rhetoric of 'freedom and democracy' ranged against 'evil doers' and Tony Blair's opinion poll ratings recovered considerably from their all-time low less than two months previously.

Meanwhile, back at the office, a discussion was taking place on email about the newly proposed Foundation Learning Tier.

> *Current developments are taking forward the Foundation Learning Tier (FLT) which will bring cohesion and clarity to all provision that sits below level 2*

> *Is this a neologism or have I just been asleep/on holiday/not paying attention? Developments in what?*

> *Why is sub-level 2 provision sitting rather than supporting or uplifting, for example?*

> *Wakey wakey! The 'Tier' describes a programme, not a qualification…and there will be elements that are non-accredited as well as things that do lead to awards within the new Framework for Achievement*

> *From a mandarinate perspective (sic)…*

> *The FLT reproduces many of the design features of the proposed new Diplomas and on the way it will subsume current E2E provision thus becoming a stepping stone to both new Diplomas and Apprenticeships or to GCSEs in due course...*

> *The FLT has moved from a tentative description, through ministerial blessing, to become part of the furniture of the sector...*

> *I hadn't realised that it had already become part of the furniture*

> *Can one spend one's learning life in the Tier?*

> *Will there be enough to keep one interested, stimulated, motivated?*

Good question. I was already wondering about the furniture on the Titanic and fiddling whilst Rome burns as I struggled to make any sense of this all too familiar exchange. At a time when a quarter of a million ordinary members of civil society in Britain marched around Edinburgh to put an end to world poverty, and whilst the repercussions of the war on terror were threatening to destroy the uneasy settlement that is British multiculturalism, the dominant discourse in adult learning – as reflected in this discussion – appeared completely disengaged from any sense of its own irrelevance.

Globaloney[2]

Since the 1990s the term globalisation has increasingly been used to describe the latest, and most advanced, development of international capitalism, made possible by the spread of new technologies. It is defined by War on Want as:

> *the way that world trade, culture and technologies have become rapidly integrated over the last twenty years, as geographic distance and cultural difference no longer pose an obstacle to trade. New technologies have increased the ease of global communication, allowing money to change hands in the blink of an eye.*

> (War on Want)

---

2   Some argue that globalisation is an ideological term that represents the victory of neo-liberal capitalism at the expense of state socialism and communism. It is seen by those who take this view as both inevitable and beneficial for humankind. Those who start from a more critical perspective and prefer to focus on resistance to neo-liberalism and the transformation of social relationships in the interests of greater equality, refer to the former position as globaloney.

It has become the organising framework within which considerable wealth is created and trade is facilitated. The national economies of the rich world and the poor world are now inter-connected as never before. We live in a globalising world characterised by increasing mutual interdependence but increasing polarisation between rich and poor within and between nations and regions. According to Zygmunt Bauman, when the world's poor are asked what aspects of their existence are most demeaning and painful, two themes 'crop up with amazing regularity – insecurity and powerlessness' (Bauman, 2001).

Globalisation is also the organising framework within which current ideas and beliefs about adult learning are given value and priority by politicians. At an earlier meeting of G8 leaders in 1999 those present issued a Charter of Aims and Ambitions for Lifelong Learning (G8 Summit, 1999).

The text faithfully reflected the emerging orthodoxy about skills and jobs that was already taking shape across Europe and North America, whilst laying bare the various common sense assumptions and apparently reasonable preoccupations – concerned with civic responsibility and social cohesion – that also enabled an all-too-easy political and professional consensus to be achieved.

In the words of the Cologne Charter, the challenge facing every country was:

> *how to become a learning society and to ensure its citizens are equipped with the knowledge, skills and qualifications they will need for the twenty first century. Economies and societies are increasingly knowledge based. Education and skills are indispensable to achieving economic success, civic responsibility and social cohesion.*

(G8 Summit, 1999)

The thinking reflected a strategic vision in which governments increasingly looked to business and the private sector to help shape appropriate educational policy and provision. The notion of a learning society was one in which individuals were to be encouraged, persuaded and cajoled into taking part in learning, in order to enhance their human, cultural and social capital, as the route to future employability, economic growth, mobility and cohesion. Whilst governments must therefore expect to expand their investment in education and training – especially in response to the needs of business and the economy – it was the responsibility of individuals to develop 'their own abilities and careers' on the basis of 'self generated learning' and by means of 'modern and effective ICT networks' and 'distance learning.'

The Charter concentrated on the 'entrepreneurial role' of education to ensure 'ready opportunities' for adult 're-skilling throughout life' as a 'passport to mobility', 'increased flexibility' and the changes taking place 'in the modern economy.' It recommended the:

continued development and improvement of internationally recognised tests to benchmark achievement...to establish clear targets in terms of higher standards and levels of achievement...and to enhance mobility in a globalised world.

(G8 Summit, 1999)

Increasingly the role of adult education, now more usually described as lifelong learning, became that of preparing flexible workers for risk and uncertainty. Competitive advantage in the global economy apparently required skills and training rather than curiosity, creativity and critical thinking.

None of which made any recognition of earlier debates that had shaped competing ideas and beliefs about the proper purpose of adult education in a changing society: radical ideas and beliefs that were concerned to reach beyond government and business interests to articulate urgent problems and pressing concerns with people *other* than professional politicians, employers and educational providers.

The legacy of Cologne, and the policy developments that flowed from it, means that, as broadly based adult education services are being dismantled and liberal adult and community education programmes are being cut, the concentration on skills is now the preferred way of ensuring that the behaviour of individuals is in tune with the brave new world of entrepreneurial consumerism. It means the onus is very firmly on individuals to take personal responsibility for their own self-improvement, in economic and social circumstances over which they have very little control.

It's a focus that makes no mention of persistent inequalities. In Britain, whilst government figures reveal only limited success of piecemeal initiatives concerned to create greater equality of opportunity, less poverty and more social justice, rhetorical conviction still attaches to schemes that are designed to counter social exclusion via personal growth and social development. A report produced by the Downing Street Strategy Unit in 2004 confirms that during the past twenty years, the incomes of better-off Britons have risen faster than those of other groups, the poorest fifth pay more of their income in taxes than the richest fifth, and the gap between the two has actually increased since New Labour came to power (Aldridge, 2004). A middle class child is currently 15 times more likely to stay middle class than a working class child is likely to move up into the middle class. A baby's fate is fixed at 22 months: school comes too late. Only the US among western nations has less upward social mobility than the UK. This is a challenging analysis given that other similar countries – Finland, France and Sweden, for example – are doing much better. But although the social and economic gap between those who thrive, and those who merely survive or go to the wall, is well documented, this does little to detract from the conventional wisdom that individuals must be encouraged to defy structural inequalities and constraints through their active demonstration of educational motivation and personal determination.

New Labour, New Learning

The conceptual and material journey from adult education to skills has not only been a linguistic odyssey. Just as few people use the same language anymore, it is increasingly difficult to find anyone working in adult education that still actively supports radical educational concerns. Over the last twenty years or so, civil society has lost its dedicated resource for emancipatory learning, in exchange for a professional community of practice, mandated by government, to deliver a centralised vision of planned social engineering. The dependence on funding from government departments and government agencies, in the context of government initiatives and targets, ensures that modern day managers and practitioners now routinely toe the line.

The changing nature of modern capitalism lies at the root of these changes. Just as the IMF and the World Bank force indigenous governments in the Global South to give up radical and popular education policies, intended to help those dying from starvation, in return for aid, so too, the dismantling of state welfare systems in the more affluent North, in favour of privatised and de-regulated alternatives, is forcing education providers in all countries to operate according to capitalist economic principles and as instruments of social engineering.

In Britain the skills agenda is closely associated with the economic requirements that derive from globalisation. In 1997, when New Labour took office, its vision for what was then called lifelong learning was already in preparation. *The Learning Age* promised an expansive agenda shaped by the requirements of a knowledge-based economy (DEE, 1998). Its emerging policy ideas on the domestic front promised 'Education, Education, Education', the reduction of poverty and the need for greater social cohesion in the interests of economic prosperity.

By 2001, the establishment of the Learning and Skills Council was intended to achieve a 'cultural revolution' in (English) attitudes to post-16 education. In its remit letter dated 9th November, 2000, David Blunkett reinforced his view that, 'we must ensure that lifelong learning becomes a battering ram against exclusion as well as a motor for economic regeneration.' In 2003 the White Paper *21st Century Skills* set out the long-term goals for raising skill levels across the nation and the strategies intended to achieve these ambitions (DES, 2003).

Increasingly then – some would say, relentlessly – the notion of adult education, rooted in broader definitions of learning to do with curiosity and passion, the development of critical intelligence, social justice and active citizenship has given way to an increasingly narrow, instrumental and utilitarian concentration on skills and knowledge for the labour market. The most recent FE White Paper (2006) serves only to consolidate this position. 'When subjected to closer inspection, much of the policy interest in lifelong learning is in fact preoccupied with the development of a more productive and efficient workforce' (Field, 2000).

However education for employment is only half the story. What happens to those who do not benefit from increasing prosperity? The Cologne Charter also addressed itself briefly to 'the needs of the disadvantaged', 'civic responsibility' and 'social cohesion' in ways that assume consensus but without any recognition of the considerable ideological and actual disagreement about the meanings of these terms and the values underpinning their realisation. As a general rule of thumb, the 'socially excluded' are always labelled collectively, but approached individually. The attention is directed to first rung, self-help and individual responsibilities, all of which underestimate the impact of structural constraints and overlook the huge disparity in resources available to different social groups – both of which affect their capacities to change their circumstances on an individual basis.

When he was Secretary of State for Education and Employment, David Blunkett became convinced that:

> lifelong learning (was) essential to sustaining a civilised and cohesive society, in which people (could) develop as active citizens, where creativity (would be) fostered and communities (could) be given practical support to overcome generations of disadvantage.

> (Blunkett, 1999)

Tony Blair was keen to endorse this view. In the run up to the 2001 election he insisted that it was 'the duty' of individuals 'to make the most of the chances they get' and declared 'individual responsibility' to be 'the key to social order' (Blair, 2001). He also took the view that what individuals cannot be persuaded to do voluntarily, they must be obliged to do as a condition of benefit, employment and citizenship. Rising moral panic in recent years about 'feral youth', binge drinking, crime and migration have all attracted summary justice responses via Blair's populist right wing enthusiasm for measures that can be administered through enforced education.

The increasingly coercive tendency of government interventions are evident, for example, in the recent Skills White Paper which contains proposals to compel welfare benefit claimants to have their basic skills needs assessed and, if they are judged inadequate, to be forced into mandatory training at the risk of losing their income. In the same vein the 2002 Nationality, Immigration and Asylum Act has determined that anyone applying for naturalisation must be assessed in terms of their language skills, required to take part in citizenship classes and to pass a citizenship test which demonstrates their knowledge of British history, traditions, politics and social structure.

At the same time family learning becomes even more sinister with the introduction of compulsory parent education classes for those – mothers, usually – whose children are causing a nuisance or found to be playing truant. For a growing number of people – particularly those who are in paid employment (because of regulatory frameworks, statutory requirements, contract compliance and customer or client expectations) or who are unemployed (because of Benefit and New Deal requirements), or who are presumed 'at risk of social exclusion' or believed to exhibit 'anti-social behaviour' – much of what adult learning describes as 'individual and social development' and/or 'opportunity and knowledge' has become increasingly obligatory (Field, 2001).

This is a very different version of active citizenship to the one independently articulated on the streets of Edinburgh during the G8 Summit. For those working in adult education, active citizenship is one of the formerly radical terms that also used to be associated with audacious grass roots energy, participatory democracy and social change. It has now become a meaningless sound bite – like empowerment, participation, social inclusion and most recently, respect – that New Labour routinely appropriates to pretend a radical sounding approach to an otherwise authoritarian pre-occupation with micro-managing the potentially troublesome attitudes of the lower orders.

Used by government ministers it usually attaches to a populist refrain, pitched at the prejudices of middle-England, about the responsibilities of those being offered the opportunity to improve themselves by their own endeavours. It is predicated on the presumption of disorderly communities, in need of some kind of behaviour modification to become 'more like us.' It is backed up with Antisocial Behaviour Orders, the biggest prison population in Europe and more than 3,000 new criminal offences added to the statute books since 1997, over half of which were never discussed in parliament, and which reflect an illiberal belief in heavy-handed regulation and an obsession with controlling the minutiae of everyday life (Morris, 2006). It is a context in which young Black Britons are more likely to go to jail than go to university.

Policies such as these are never used to coerce the middle classes into learning. No-one wonders whether those who live next door to me eat a healthy diet, put their children to bed at a reasonable hour, drink to excess or suffer from low self-esteem. In my neighbourhood we don't have to participate in local meetings to prove that we are good citizens. We pay our taxes and expect those whose job it is to sort out the street lighting, the rubbish collections and the road repairs to get on with it.

There are two dangers in this modernising – and somewhat moralising – tendency, which seems to regard society as an aggregation of individuals, who are invariably referred to individually as solitary rather than social agents. Not only does it relegate discussions about common struggles and common interests to the dustbin of history, but it also translates aspirations for democratic renewal and critical engagement with political processes into issues of self-fulfilment, confidence building, consumer choice, employability and volunteering (Blunkett, 2001). It also appears to require participation in ways that are determined to adjust the socially excluded to the norms and values of white middle-class society – through education, re-training, volunteering, voting – in ways that rely on more than a little coercion and which tolerate few excuses from those who don't want to participate in this way. The danger here is that the blame for social exclusion and poverty is placed on apathetic or wilful non-participating individuals rather than on wider structural and societal trends and influences.

But it's a strategy that does little to win hearts and minds. The latest NIACE survey of participation in adult learning (Aldridge & Tuckett, 2006) reveals that fewer people are currently engaged in learning than when the present government came to power. The latest evidence from the Learning and Skills Council shows that in 2005-6 participation in further education fell by between 10 per cent and 26 per cent in every age range above nineteen. At the same time there was a decline of 10 per cent in adult and community learning (Tuckett, 2007). However prescriptive and instrumental the learning agenda has become, we can draw some comfort from the fact that its actual grip on most peoples lived reality is minimal. In this kind of policy climate, with this kind of professional compliance, the sort of adult education that once called itself a movement, that in the words of Raymond Williams should be a resource to ordinary people for a journey of hope, has been cut off at its roots.

If You Can't Change the World, Change Yourself!

Marx was right when he insisted that the ruling ideas of any age are the ideas of the ruling class. He also made it clear that the purpose of education is not simply to understand the world but to change it. In a recent poll conducted by BBC Radio 4's *In our time* programme, one half of those taking part thought that Karl Marx was the most important philosopher of all time. But his popularity with the chattering classes has done little to establish the significance of his insights in contemporary discussions about adult learning.

For the most part adult learning has given up on teaching an understanding of the world, let alone trying to change it. And with corporate capitalism in charge on a global scale, supported by sympathetic governments from the North, it is not so surprising – if you go along with Marx – that free market consumerism, new managerialism, militarism and competitive individualism have become the big ideas that help to keep the masses in their place. In this kind of climate, there is little official room – in the West, at any rate – for grand narratives, and every encouragement for the belief that because you can't change the world, you must strive to change yourself.

The idea that adult learning can help feckless and potentially disruptive individuals to change their ways is not new. Writing in *Adult Education for a Change* twenty-five years ago, Nell Keddie pointed out that educational

> *provision for the disadvantaged…conspicuously avoids any mention of*
> *social class and…is contexted…within a social pathology which separates*
> *the problems presented by individuals from the social and political order which*
> *creates these problems.*

(Keddie, 1980)

In the same publication, writing about disadvantage, I drew attention to the ways in which:

> *the language of 'personal deficit', 'affliction' and the need for 'treatment' to*
> *'rehabilitate' the 'malfunctioning' adult into 'normal' society (ran) like a medical*
> *checklist through the literature of adult education.*

(Thompson, 1980b)

It was a view that saturated the writing of influential pundits of the time such as Peter Clyne (1972) and Henry Arthur Jones (1972, 1979) and which formed the basis of their advice to the Russell Committee (1973) in what subsequently became known as 'Russell category work.'

The ideology of disadvantage served to hold large sections of the working class personally responsible for their own misfortunes by making it seem as though unemployment, poverty, poor education and slum conditions were *the consequence* of individual deficiencies, family breakdown and cultural deprivation. To sustain the ideology, victims were discovered all over the place but especially among 'the isolated' and 'apathetic' residents of vast council estates, prisoners' wives, ethnic minorities and single parents, all identified by their 'obvious inadequacy' and beloved by those involved in basic education and 'Russell category work' (Thompson, 1980b).

Because most adult educators – then, just as now – were liberal in their disposition, ideas about disadvantage connected to the belief that education could lead its victims towards 'spiritual fulfilment', 'personhood' and 'social integration' (Paterson, 1979). The ideas of Carl Rogers and Abraham Maslow lent dubious psychological credibility to notions of 'self actualisation' (Maslow, 1968, 1970) and 'becoming a person' (Rogers, 1961). But despite the veneer of liberalism, Maslow constantly contrasted ordinary people 'who need others' with self actualising people who do not. He identified human needs hierarchically, with food and shelter at the bottom, and self-actualisation – defined as autonomy and not needing others – at the top. Self actualising people were those who could 'make up their own minds, come to their own decisions…(be) responsible for themselves and their own destinies.' They were obviously superior to those 'who have their minds made up for them' and who were 'apt to feel helpless, weak and totally determined', those who were 'the prey for predators, flabby whiners, rather than self determining persons' (Maslow, 1968).

What Maslow described as 'self actualising' Rogers called 'becoming a person.' He meant by it the capacity to achieve emotional self sufficiency and the determination to pursue one's own individually defined goals. The implication was that a process of personal change and individual effort could lead to individual liberation and fulfilment – and ultimately – the abolition of nasty things like poverty or sexual and racial oppression, because having become a person, individuals would not let themselves be anymore affected by such concerns. On one occasion he claimed that the troubles in Northern Ireland could be solved if only sufficient trained humanistic counsellors would go there and hold encounter groups on every street corner (Grimshaw, 1986). It is not only history that has called into question the naivety of such views.

It may seem surprising that ideas of this kind were so inspirational to adult educators in the 1970s. They are certainly illuminating about the intellectual and ideological climate in which stereotypical descriptions contributed to pathological definitions of disadvantage, leading to arguments in favour of behaviour modification through education, rather than wealth and educational redistribution, for example, in favour of the poor. In her excellent study of class and gender Beverley Skeggs is sceptical about what she calls the 'psy' professions, whose prominence she sees as directly related to the lack of attention given to social class over the last twenty years and to the emergence of 'an authorising narrative of personal trauma in which singular difficult experiences come to account for the whole personality' in ways that do not constitute a liberating ideology (Skeggs, 1997).

In similar vein, a recent article in *Adults Learning* by Kathryn Ecclestone revisits some familiar territory in the light of more recent trends and emerging orthodoxies. She is worried that the growing popularity of psycho-therapeutic notions such as self esteem and emotional intelligence – beloved by women's magazines, reality TV and self-help manuals – have now gone mainstream:

leading to new professional activities in emotional management, life coaching, mentoring, counselling and interventions to build self esteem and make people feel good emotionally in the pursuit of motivation, educational achievement and social inclusion.

(Ecclestone, 2004)

She is right to be concerned.

In the popular wisdom of adult education practice it is certainly the case that ideas about confidence, emotional intelligence and self-esteem are commonplace. The literature of funding applications, project reports and evaluation exercises are full of claims by policy makers and practitioners alike that interventions targeted at so-called non traditional learners and socially excluded groups give rise to increased confidence and self esteem (Eldred, 2005) I had thought that this was an essentially western phenomenon until I read recently in Sierra Leone – a small West African country emerging from eleven years of civil war with a ranking of last in the world in the Human Development Index – that:

the experience of social exclusion from decision-making bodies and processes, the lack of educational opportunities, early marriage and the demands of childbearing and rearing cause many women and young people to suffer from low self-esteem and a lack of confidence *[my emphasis] in their judgement.*

(Von Kotze, 2005)

This must surely be the language of the writer rather than the assessment of the women and young people in question but indicates just how pervasive – even in the context of extreme poverty and genocide – this spurious discourse has become.

Back in Britain it is no coincidence that the language of self-esteem and emotional literacy resonate with broader cultural and political preoccupations. According to Ecclestone (2004), 'there is a growing tone in policy circles that managing one's emotions, having good self-esteem and being emotionally literate…are part of the responsibilities of being a good citizen.' According to Nick Emler (2001), on the basis of his substantial review of the theoretical and empirical evidence for self-esteem, so strong is this new orthodoxy in political and educational circles, you would think 'low self-esteem is the cause of all the problems in all the world.'

It is easy to see why educational practitioners are attracted to ideas that seem to focus on students' personal and emotional development in an apparently supportive and benign way, despite the fact that there is little agreement about what self esteem actually is and virtually no convincing evidence about its effects or whether interventions designed to 'raise it' actually work (Ecclestone 2004; Emler, 2001). As a form of professional responsibility it no doubt helps to counter the overly bureaucratic, instrumental and target driven culture that adult learning has become. The government regards it as both the cause and effect of social exclusion and welcomes any amount of short-term interventions designed to counter the dysfunctional and negative behaviour of those who do not have enough of it. The belief that developing confidence and self-esteem can remedy a wide range of personal and social problems helps to distract attention from the structural causes of inequality, institutional and actual racism and from the widening gap between rich and poor more generally. And of course, it plays to the prejudices of a profession that is already well used to labelling and stereotyping its students.

What is to be Done?

When the current state of lifelong learning gets written about by future historians you have to wonder what they will make of it all. Debates in the recent past might well have been contentious and fiercely contested but at least they involved political discussion – at all levels – about ideas and purpose. And they led to a lively mix of liberal and radical education in both formal and non-formal contexts. Whatever else, education was a resource that people in communities of interest could use to both enrich and change their lives.

These days, instead of specialist teachers and enthusiasts teaching an extensive range of subjects, to a relatively wide range of people, the day job for most of us entails enticing and cajoling the poor and other minorities into remedial activities designed to make them healthier, more socially competent and more likely to get a job. Either that or processing the blizzard of paperwork routinely required to prove that the latest short term initiative has been delivered on time, on budget, and in line with government targets. Either way, we know that large numbers of potential students are voting with their feet.

What counts as adult learning has come to rely on project workers, mentors and cheer leaders, drumming up support for the new managerialist desire for well behaved, gainfully employed and respectful people; with learning goals that are said to be good for them and good for society expressed in the language of skills and self esteem. It's a model that reduces teaching to the role of life coach and is based on the implicit presumption that if you can't change the world, better change yourself to make the best of it. It doesn't leave much room for dissent or wondering what to do about climate change and world poverty.

What is really good for society, of course, is that despite all the dumbing down and bossing about and 'rolling out of strategies', ordinary people are increasingly making their voices heard on their own terms in other ways. The sheer breadth and energy of civil society movements, as we have seen, are a powerful and optimistic recognition of the belief in citizen action and solidarity beyond national boundaries. But the issues involved are complex and contested. As capital has gone global it has served to undermine the sovereignty of the nation state, whilst putting pressure on rich countries and poor countries alike to maximise profit and cut back on public expenditure. The same processes are at work that get called modernisation in the rich world and structural adjustment in the poor world – the costs of which, in both contexts, are more likely to be borne by those who can afford them least. Questions and legitimate grievances abound but solutions are in short supply. Social movements may pursue regressive as well as progressive goals, just as they may lead to the incorporation of dissent by the state rather than the challenging of inequality and social justice.

Lifelong learning is central to these concerns whether we like it or not. As employees of the state, we still have political choices to make about being part of the problem or part of the solution. This means engaging with ideas and purpose, not simply process and management.

In my view it is time to get back in touch with the energy, commitment and creative anger that fuels civil society in its quest for global justice and which rediscovers the educational potential and significance of popular social movements. We know that knowledge grows best when it is created through dialogue and social interaction, and when it is spread around (Crowther, 2005). Sharing a common purpose with others about issues that matter, and which are national and international in their repercussions, is both exhilarating and socially responsible, in ways that the individualised quest for self-improvement is not. Taking action makes you think. It makes you challenge what is usually taken for granted. Acquiring insight leads to more questions. Finding answers is the stuff of reason, investigation, communication, inspiration and social change.

The search for answers might be artistic, practical, theoretical. The expression of critical thinking does not need esoteric language or the proliferation of qualifications but it does need dedicated teachers who can make relevant and practical connections in imaginative and democratic ways. The kinds of knowledge that education can help to produce and contribute to better understanding is the essential ingredient a democracy needs if it is to flourish and continually re-invent itself from one generation to the next. The popular creation of knowledge, linked to social action, makes sense in a troubled world because supporting a campaign or joining a movement is a powerful way of learning through experience and making history, rather than simply enduring it. It is precisely this kind of informal learning that fuels the desire for more knowledge-making and more actively democratic societies (McGivney, 1999).

And as a result, well-informed and more knowledgeable citizens are better equipped to take responsible and effective action on their own behalf. They are more likely to hold their leaders to account for the policies and actions they take – including their response to global poverty. When the current state of adult learning gets written about by future historians, it is hard to imagine a more important contribution we could have made.

References

Aldridge, F. & Tuckett, A. (2006). *Green shoots? The NIACE survey on adult participation in learning.* Leicester: NIACE.

Aldridge, S. (2004). *Life chances and social mobility: An overview of the evidence.* Government Strategy Unit Report. London: Government Strategy Unit.

Bauman, Z. (2001, 29 December). Quality and inequality. *Guardian Saturday Review.*

Blair, T. (2001, 8 February). The Government's agenda for the future. Speech.*URL: http:// www.number-10.gov.uk/output/Page1579.asp*

Blunkett, D. (1999). *The learning and skills council prospectus: Learning to succeed.* London: HMSO.

Blunket, D. (2001, 7 February). From strength to strength: Rebuilding the community through voluntary action. Speech to Annual Conference of National Council for Voluntary Organisations. *URL: http://www.dfes.gov.uk/speeches/media/documents/ strengthtostrength.doc*

Clyne, P. (1972). *The disadvantaged adult.* London: Longman.

Crowther, J., Galloway, V. & Martin, I. (Eds.). (2005). *Engaging the academy: International Perspectives.* Leicester: NIACE.

Department for Education and Employment. (1998). *The learning age: A renaissance for a new Britain.* London: HMSO.

Department for Education and Skills. (2003). *21st Century skills: Realising our potential.* London: The Stationery Office.

Ecclestone, K. (2004). Developing self esteem and emotional well-being: Inclusion or intrusion? *Adults Learning, 16*(3), 11-13.

Eldred, J., Dutton, N., Snowdon, K. & Ward, J. (2005). Catching confidence. *Adults Learning, 16*(8), 29-31.

Emler, N. (2001). *Self-esteem: The costs and causes of low self worth.* York: Joseph Rowntree Foundation.

Field, J. (2000). *Lifelong learning and the new education order.* Stoke-on-Trent: Trentham.

Field, J. (2001). *Lifelong learning and social inclusion.* In F. Coffield (Ed.), What progress are we making with lifelong learning? The evidence from research. Newcastle: University of Newcastle.

Freire, P. (1972). *Pedagogy of the oppressed.* London: Penguin.

G8 Summit. (1999, 18-25 June). *Cologne Charter: Aims and ambitions for lifelong learning.* Adopted by G8 at 25th Economic Summit, Cologne. *URL: http://www.g8. utoronto.ca/summit/1999koln/charter.htm*

Grimshaw, J. (1986). *Feminist philosophers: Women's perspectives on philosophical traditions.* Brighton: Wheatsheaf.

Jones, H.A. (1972). Foreword. *The disadvantaged adult.* London: Longman.

Jones, H.A. (1979). *A strategy for the basic education of adults.* ACACE.

Jubilee 2000 Coalition. (2000). *The world will never be the same again.* London: Jubilee 2000 Coalition.

Keddie, N. (1980). *Adult education: An ideology of individualism.* In J. Thompson (Ed.), Adult education for a change. London: Hutchinson.

McGivney, V. (1999). *Informal learning in the community: A trigger for change and development.* Leicester: NIACE.

Maslow, A. (1968). *Towards a psychology of being.* Princeton: Van Nostrand.

Maslow, A. (1970). *Motivation and personality.* New York: Harper & Row.

Mayo, M. (2005). *Global citizens: Social movements and the challenge of globalisation.* London: Zed Books.

Morris, N. (2006, 16 August). Blair's frenzied law making: A new offence for everyday spent in office. *The Independent.*

Naidoo, K. (2005). Secretary General of CIVICUS: World Alliance for Citizen Participation. Personal communication.

Paterson, R. W. K. (1979). *Values, education and the adult.* London: Routledge & Kegan Paul.

Rogers, C. (1961). *On being a person.* London: Constable.

Russell. E.L. (1973). *Adult education: A plan for development.* The Russell Report. London: HMSO.

Skeggs, B. (1997). *Formations of class and gender.* London: Sage.

Taking Liberties Collective. (1989). *Learning the hard way: Women's oppression in men's education.* London: Macmillan.

Thompson, J. (Ed.). (1980a). *Adult education for a change.* London: Hutchinson.

Thompson, J. (1980b). Adult education and the disadvantaged. In J. Thompson, *Adult education for a change.* London: Macmillan.

Thompson, J. (1983). *Learning liberation: Women's response to men's education.* London: Croom Helm.

Thompson, J. (2000). *Women, class and education.* London: Routledge.

Thompson, J. (2005). Learning and doing. *Adults Learning, 16*(10), 11-12.

Tuckett, A. (2007, 2 January). Leitch cannot disguise the death of lifelong learning. *Guardian*.

Von Kotze, A. (2005). Are we all together? *Adults Learning 16*(10), 14-16.

Waltzer, M. (1992). The civil society argument. In C. Mouffe (Ed.), *Dimensions of radical democracy*, (pp. 89-107). London: Verso.

War on Want. *URL: http://www.globalworkplace.com*

Is Adult Education
a Discipline?

RICHARD TAYLOR
CAMBRIDGE UNIVERSITY

Is Adult Education a Discipline?

RICHARD TAYLOR
CAMBRIDGE UNIVERSITY

Introduction

There is a hierarchy of disciplines, as there are of institutions, in UK higher education and in most developed countries. Of course, the nature of the hierarchy – and of the perceived substantive content – of disciplinary areas has changed markedly over the centuries. It is not my intention here to enter into this historical evolution, interesting area though that is. Rather, this paper begins by discussing the nature of 'academic disciplines' in contemporary western societies, focussing primarily upon the UK. This is an area of some contention in contemporary academic contexts, largely for two, related, reasons: first, the development of deconstructionist and postmodern analysis generally has had a profound and unsettling effect upon conceptions of epistemology in the academy, and this has had a direct impact upon definitions of 'disciplines'; secondly, the rapid expansion of higher education and the increasing emphasis upon vocationalism and 'performativity' have resulted in a large increase in the number of subject areas and programmes now regarded as legitimate in the higher education context. These issues are examined below, and this leads on to a more focussed discussion on inter-disciplinarity and the nature of the relationship between the broad field of 'education' and the specific area of 'adult education.'

This will enable some tentative answer to the question as to whether, in the contemporary context of higher education, **adult** education has legitimacy as an identifiable discipline.

The Contemporary Debates over 'Knowledge' and 'Disciplines'

Whatever the changes in the definitions of disciplines in the academy over the last one hundred years or so, there has been no period in which education has had, to put it kindly, an elevated position in the hierarchy. If this is the case for education, it is doubly so for adult education.

This specific issue is situated necessarily in the overall socio-political environment of the university in society. This is a large canvas: all I would do here is to draw attention to the definitive contemporary analysis of these questions by Gerard Delanty (2001), Ronald Barnett (1990, 1997, 2000), Tony Becher and Paul Trowler (2002) and Peter Scott (1995, 1997, 2000), and to summarise some of the points relevant to the specific question here.

Around the turn of the nineteenth and twentieth centuries it was clear that, in the UK, the old liberal notion of the university, epitomised by Cardinal Newman and giving primacy to 'natural theology and the spiritual value of knowledge' (Delanty, 2001, p. 23) had been superseded by a conception of the university and its disciplines that was more appropriate to a mass society. 'Fact' and 'value' became more distinct; professional and direct economic relevance became more dominant criteria in establishing the legitimacy of disciplinary knowledge; and, most important of all perhaps in our context, there was an increase in the sharp differentiation between disciplines and the idea that specialist disciplinary knowledge must be developed to meet specific, expert needs in an ever more complex society.

A more or less positivist methodology became dominant, along with an assumption that 'scientific rationalism' was now unchallengeable, epistemologically as well as economically. To cite Delanty again: 'The twentieth century was an era of the expert, and professional society replaced the last remnants of the Enlightenment humanism' (2001, p. 24). In one sense, the dominant **disciplinary** frameworks reflected the newly dominant **occupational** groups and their needs for focussed expertise on relevant technological and professional skills (Perkin, 1989). As with all such changes, this was not a neat and complete change of course: the 'old', central disciplinary concerns remained but they were complemented if not challenged by new subjects and disciplinary frameworks.

All this has been fundamentally challenged since the 1980s. Linked ideas about post-Fordism, post-industrialism, and globalisation (Scott, 1998; Smith & Webster, 1997), the ideas of both scientific rationalism *per se* (and its methodology) and accompanying notions of 'objective truth' have come under sustained attack. The old notions of disciplines have foundered; no longer is it accepted that there are disciplines with specific and separate methodologies and with acknowledged boundaries, united in their assumptions about empirical method and the criteria for establishing 'truth.' This has been linked, in turn, to the undermining of the so-called 'grand-narratives': in the main, critique has been directed at socio-political ideologies and their accompanying political practice – in particular socialism. However, in the context of the academy this has been coupled with an attack on disciplinary legitimacy and the 'liberal progressivism' which, it is held, have characterised implicitly the prevailing academic orthodoxy.

This is not the place to discuss critically such arguments: elsewhere I have attempted to argue strongly against this postmodern analysis as both intellectually erroneous and politically, in the end, conservative (Taylor, et al., 2002). The point here is rather to note this development and its connection with the new prominence of subject areas which are characterised by their vocational, competence and performativity orientations. Thus, for good or ill, a whole series of disciplines had been added to the canon of the academy in the latter years of the twentieth century. These include, clearly, business studies, communication and media studies, performing arts, environmental studies, computer studies and industrial studies. This is a somewhat selective list, of course: in particular it does not address the important additions in the sciences and engineering fields.

My argument is, however, that it is clear that the definition in the academy of 'discipline' per se has changed fundamentally. To be sure, the 'central disciplines' of traditional structures remain: the physical sciences, the life sciences, the main arts disciplines – English literature, history and the rest (though it should be noted that the absolute core arts disciplines of the past – notably classics, philosophy and, to an extent theology – have declined markedly in size and importance). But the **trend** is towards **applied** disciplines, and moreover to **interdisciplinarity**.

It is worth noting that, neither in principle nor in practice, does this entail a particular political or ideological slant. Critics of postmodernity, including many on the left, have argued that the postmodern position leads to 'conservatism' at a number of levels. Whether or not his is the case, the arrival of new disciplines that are regarded as legitimate does not, clearly, herald a uniform move to a new academic conservatism. There are several areas – industrial studies, environmental studies, peace studies and many others – which have implications, other things being equal, of progressive orientation.

To return to the main theme: this new disciplinary paradigm is accompanied by what Michael Gibbons and his colleagues have described as a new epistemological structure, encompassing 'Mode 1 and Mode 2' knowledge production.

Gibbons argues that Mode 1 has been based essentially upon rationalist methods and assumptions. That is, knowledge production has been linear, consensual and cumulative, and it has been a **closed** system in that it was self-referential within specialised scientific communities. Moreover, and importantly, the academic communities concerned argued that for reasons of principle as well as practice, scientific research had to be funded from public sources.

'Mode 2' knowledge, on the other hand, is, in Peter Scott's words:

> *multi-variant, unsystematic and even anti-coherent. The source of innovation is to be found not only, or even especially, in the laboratory…indeed it is most likely to arise in the often contested borderland between the university and the market/society. As a result technology is not subordinated to, or a derivative of, science. It is an autonomous terrain.*

(Scott, 1995, p. 144)

Scott goes on to note other characteristics of Mode 2 knowledge, including its open nature and crucially its interplay with organisations and cultures **outside** the academy. There is, it might be added, a resultant emphasis upon application, practicality and usefulness in contemporary commercial contexts.

Higher education in developed societies is thus a much more complex and diverse (as well as larger) system than in the past. Whether this is good or bad, coherent or chaotic, supportive of progressive social development or the reverse, and so on, is of course a separate issue, or series of issues, which I do not intend to enter into here. This, I would argue, provides the essential context for a discussion of 'adult education' as a discipline. The emergence of a group of new professional areas of study and their acceptance as disciplines in the latter decades of the twentieth century provides an opportunity for adult education to establish itself as 'legitimate' in a way which was simply not possible before. As Harold Perkin (1989; 1996) has argued, twentieth century society in the West has been characterised by the rise of a credentialed professionalism. And it has been the academy that has, increasingly, provided the accreditation, or validation of professional bodies supplying the accreditation. So for some decades now, the newer professions of, for example, education, social work, computer science, and urban planning, have become accepted as disciplinary areas, and added to the historical payers of existing professional disciplines such as architecture and the various brands of engineering.

One obvious common feature of all such professional areas – education, social work and the rest – is that they are inter-disciplinary area studies. That is, the focus is upon the theory and practice of a particular professional area, and this study is informed by a number of relevant disciplines. In the case of social work, for example, the major disciplines involved are psychology, sociology, social policy and law – with arguably 'ancillary' inputs from history, political studies, counselling and so on.

Moreover, all these areas are characterised to a greater or lesser extent by an emphasis upon Gibbon's Mode 2 knowledge.

How does adult education fit into this pattern? Assuming that it can be asserted, given the foregoing discussion, that education *per se* is a legitimate discipline in the sense of being focussed, inter-disciplinary area, the obvious question is the extent to which 'adult education' should be seen as a subsidiary branch of 'education', in an analogous way to primary or secondary education or whatever. At one level this is clearly the case. Despite the ill-fated attempt to differentiate approaches to learning for adults – Knowles's andragogy – it is clear that adult education as a discipline is concerned, as is other educational study, with the psychological processes involved in learning, the sociological environment in which such learning takes place and the alternatives there might be to present practices and priorities. In that sense, education as a whole could be regarded as, more or less, a seamless robe. Moreover, there can surely be no question but that adult education in this sense is an absolutely legitimate part of the spectrum of education.

However, that is not the end of the discussion. There is arguably clear blue water between the focus **and the culture** of 'education' concerned as it primarily if not exclusively with the education and learning of children within the compulsory system, and 'adult education' whose concerns are different and diverse – but have no involvement whatever with the education of children in the compulsory system.

Above and beyond this clear divergence, adult education has both a long and very particular history: and a strong, though complex contested, culture (Fieldhouse, 1996). Because adult education spans the whole post-compulsory sectors, it has attracted a range of specialisms and perspectives. Thus, its practitioner's range in focus from those concentrating upon literacy, numeracy and basic skills through to those engaged with post-doctoral and/or post-experience continuing professional development provision (at full cost plus) for high status professionals – and everything in between. At the risk of over simplification, or indeed ideological reductionism, it is perhaps possible to identify the following main trusts of adult education concerns:

- Liberal education for personal development, following Newman, and within adult education itself Albert Mansbridge and the more liberal proponents of the early WEA (Fieldhouse, 1977; Ryan 1999; Wallis & Mee, 1983; Newman).

- Part-time, credit bearing study for adult learners, leading to awards such as part-time degrees.

- Social purpose, community education, with a clearly radical political ethos seeing education as linked to empowerment (Lovett, 1983, 1988; Ward & Taylor, 1986; Fieldhouse, 1977; Thompson, 2000).

- Vocational education, linked to governmental and (some) employer priorities for education and training as necessary for economic, human capital reasons (Coffield, 1997, 1999a, 1999b).

Of course, these approaches are not discreet: indeed, governments and the EU would argue that they are complementary – or at least the first, second and fourth are! (Taylor, et al., 2002). Whatever view is taken of this, there is, clearly, a wide spectrum here. All perspectives are united, though, in their concern with learning in all its environments **beyond** the compulsory system.

In the large majority of provision, the primary concern is with those large numbers of adults in **all** Western societies who have not had the benefit of higher education. (The main exception, of course is CPD work in higher education.) There is some commonality, too, in curricular and pedagogic approaches across the spectrum of adult education. Virtually all adult education settings involve small group, seminar work, where tutor is the part facilitator, in part academic, drawing on the groups' 'life experience', and accompanying varying levels of ability, educational background and so on. Edward Thompson, a great adult tutor as well as an outstanding intellectual figure of the second half of the twentieth century, put this point well in a lecture in 1968:

> All education which is worth the name involves a relationship of mutuality, a dialectic: and no worthwhile educationalist conceives of his material as a class of inert recipients of instruction. But, in liberal adult education, no tutor is likely to last out a session – and no class is likely to stay the course with him – if he is under the misapprehension that the role of the class is passive. What is different about the adult student is the experience which he brings to the relationship. This experience modifies, sometimes subtly and sometimes more radically, the entire educational process... To strike the balance between intellectual rigour and respect for the experience is always difficult. But the balance today (1968) is seriously awry...(I wish to redress it a little) by reminding us that universities engage in adult education not only to teach but also to learn...

(Thompson, 1968)

There is thus a strong case, in my view, for there being an identifiable disciplinary area for adult education in its own right. There is, moreover, one further crucial argument in support of this contention in the contemporary context. In all Western European developed societies – and in Anglophone societies in other parts of the world including North America, Australia and New Zealand – 'adult education' has become broadened into the much more high profile concept of 'lifelong learning' (Coffield, 1999b; Barnett, 2000; Watson & Taylor, 1998; Field & Leicester, 2000; Field, 2000; Schuetze & Slowey, 2000).

Arguably, at least in principle, lifelong learning by definition embraces the whole lifespan. But certainly at present, adult education – or rather the learning that takes place in all its forms subsequent to the end of compulsory school education – is at the heart of lifelong learning; similarly, the relevant expertise and commitment in universities and elsewhere, in terms of practice and research, resides centrally with 'adult educators.' The academy as a whole, as government, is now fully committed to lifelong learning, however defined (Taylor, et al., 2002). The discussion of lifelong learning thus permeates the academy: in many respects, lifelong learning, and thus adult education, is the catalyst and the core from which the emerging new higher education may develop.

References

Barnett, R. (1990). *The idea of a university.* Buckingham: SRHE and Open University Press.

Barnett, R. (1997). *Higher education: A critical business.* Buckingham: SRHE and Open University Press.

Barnett, R. (2000). *Realizing the university in an age of supercomplexity.* Buckingham: SRHE and Open University Press.

Barnett, R. & Griffin, A. (1997). *The end of knowledge in higher education.* London: Cassell.

Beecher, T. & Trowler, P.R. (2002). *Academic tribes and territories: Intellectual enquiry and the cultures of disciplines* (2nd ed.). Buckingham: SRHE and Open University Press.

Coffield, F. (1997). *Can the UK become a learning society?* Fourth Annual Adult Education Lecture, King's College, London.

Coffield, F. (1999a). *Why's the beer always strong up north? Studies of lifelong learning in Europe.* London: Policy Press.

Coffield, F. (1999b). *Breaking the consensus: Lifelong learning as social control.* Inaugural lecture, University of Newcastle.

Delanty, G. (2001). *Challenging knowledge: The university in the knowledge society.* Buckingham: SRHE and Open University Press.

Field, J. (2000). *Lifelong learning and the new educational order.* London: Trentham Books.

Field, J. & Leicester, M. (Eds.). (2000). *Lifelong learning: Education across the lifespan.* London: Routledge Falmer.

Fieldhouse, R. (1977). *The Workers' Education Association: Aims and achievements, 1903-1977.* New York: Syracuse University.

Fieldhouse, R. & Associates (1996). *A history of modern British adult education.* Leicester: NIACE.

Foucault, M. (1980). *Power/Knowledge: Selected interviews and other writings, 1972-1977.* New York: Pantheon.

Foucault, M. (1986). What is enlightenment? In P. Rainbow, *The Foucault reader.* Harmondsworth: Peregrin.

Lovett, T. (1983). *Adult education, community development and the working class.* Beckenham: Croom Helm.

Lovett, T. (Ed.). (1988). *Radical approaches to adult education: A reader.* London: Routledge.

Lyotard, J.F. (1979). *The postmodern condition: A report on knowledge,* (2nd ed.). Manchester: Manchester University Press.

Newman, J.H. *The idea of a university.*

Perkin, H. (1989). *The rise of professional society: England since 1880.* London: Routledge.

Perkin H. (1996). *Third revolution: Professional elites in the modern world.* London: Routledge.

Ryan, A. (1999). *Liberal anxieties and liberal education.* London: Profile Books.

Schuetze, H. & Slowey, M. (Eds.). (2000). *Lifelong learners in higher education: International perspectives on change.* Brighton: Falmer.

Scott, P. (1995). *The meanings of mass higher education.* Buckingham: SRHE and Open University Press.

Scott, P. (1997). The postmodern university? In A. Smith & F. Webster (Eds.), *The postmodern university? Contested visions of higher education in society.* Buckingham: SRHE and Open University Press.

Scott, P. (Ed.). *The globalisation of higher education.* Buckingham: SRHE and Open University Press.

Scott, P. (Ed.). (2000). *Higher education reformed.* Brighton: Falmer.

Smith, A. & Webster, F. (Eds.). (1997). *The postmodern university? Contested visions of higher education in society.* Buckingham: SRHE and Open University Press.

Taylor, R., Barr, J. & Steele, T. (2002). *For a radical higher education after postmodernism.* Buckingham: SRHE and Open University Press.

Thompson, E.P. (1968). Education and experience. Fifth Annual Albert Mansbridge Memorial Lecture, University of Leeds.

Thompson, J. (2000). *Stretching the academy: The politics and practices of widening participation in higher education.* Leicester: NIACE.

Wallis, J. & Mee, G. (1983). *Community schools: Claims and performance.* Nottingham: Department of Adult Education, University of Nottingham.

Ward, K. & Taylor, R. (1986). *Adult education and the working class: Education for the missing millions.* Beckenham: Croom Helm.

Watson, D. & Taylor, R. (1998). *Lifelong learning and the university: A post-Dearing agenda.* Brighton: Falmer.

Working in and with Civil Society

LYN TETT
UNIVERSITY OF EDINBURGH, SCOTLAND

Working in and with Civil Society

LYN TETT
UNIVERSITY OF EDINBURGH, SCOTLAND

Introduction: Finding Common Purpose

A healthy democracy requires a robust civil society in which a variety of constituencies are capable of making their voices heard. Currently, however, whilst there is a great deal of rhetoric about the importance of empowering learners to be more autonomous, powerful socio-economic pressures make this increasingly difficult. One of these pressures is a pervasive pessimism that issues such as 'globalisation' are beyond our control and it is impossible to protect others and ourselves from its effects. As Ferudi points out, people as increasingly seen as 'victims of their own circumstances rather than authors of their own lives. The outcome of these developments is a world that equates the good life with self-limitation and risk aversion' (Ferudi, 1997, p. 147). Belief in the power of fate, and doubts about people's ability to cope with life, undermine personal autonomy and responsibility whilst leading us to accept closer state regulation of behaviour (Ferudi, 1997).

It seems important to challenge these discourses that constrain the capability of people to take control of their own learning otherwise compliance, rather than change, will be the result. This paper seeks to examine whether the academy can make a difference to people's lives through challenging these 'victim' discourses. It will consider strategies that encourage people to take back control. One important consideration is how the ability of all citizens can be acknowledged so that people can define their own problems and find appropriate solutions. Engaging in learning can improve people's social and economic conditions and bring about positive change but being clear about our purposes is crucial. As Beresford and Croft point out, (1993, p. 9):

> The democratic approach is about more than having a voice in [education and learning], however important it is. It is also about how we are treated and regarded more generally, and with having a greater say and control over the whole of our lives.

Education that is rooted in the interests and experience of ordinary people should contribute to a more inclusive and democratic society. What are the possibilities for finding common purpose between the academy and civil society that would contribute to the difficult educational task of democratic renewal? Before considering this question let us consider what is meant by citizenship.

Citizenship

Citizenship is a difficult concept to define although there are broadly two main types of understanding. One conception sees it as a status bestowed on those people who are full members of a community with the rights and obligations that flow from that membership. Another conception attaches importance the social relationships that enable people to actively participate in decision-making in their social, economic, cultural and political life (Lister, 1997, p. 29). The first conception gives priority to the status and the second to citizenship as an active practice. This latter conception prioritises the ability of people who are disadvantaged, in terms of power and resources, to exercise their civil and political rights effectively in order to achieve their valued goals. This involves promoting their free and equal participation, in both defining the problems to be addressed and the solutions to be used, in ways that mitigate economic and social inequalities. It requires a public space in which different groups can come together to air their differences and build solidarity around common interests.

People have the fundamental right as citizens to give voice and be listened to within the process of decision-making. Members of communities need to recognise each other as citizens who share a common status and equal rights but this is difficult given that we live increasingly within communities of difference. Ours is a heterogeneous society with many different voices, which means that people can be excluded from participation in democratic decision-making in two broad ways. One way is by failing to recognise people's cultural differences and the other is through the inequality of socio-economic resources. The challenge for a strengthened democracy is to discover processes that can reconcile the valuing of difference with the need for shared understanding and agreement about public purpose that dissolves prejudice and discrimination. People's interests therefore need to be represented in public debates both in terms of their cultural conditions and their material class interests. An inclusive citizenship requires the recognition of different voices as well as the fair distribution of resources that provide the conditions for equal participation. The challenge is to establish an understanding that embraces both the recognition of people's voices and the redistribution of resources in order to create a just, inclusive democracy.

The autonomy of groups to define their own problems and develop their own organisational structures leads to a more genuinely democratic structure. The educational opportunities presented by working with such groups that are committed to progressive social change can be enormous. Working to develop a curriculum from the social context of individual and collective experience requires identifying the contradictions that experience raises. For example, the experience of being disabled includes dependency, and the analysis of what this means should be regarded as an educational resource rather than a problem to be solved. The idea of activists as learners also connects with the historical tradition of radical social action that emerged out of industrialisation and the consequential changes in social structures in which political analysis was regarded as a prerequisite for transformative social change. Educational engagement with dissenting citizens poses quite starkly the choice of developing an enriched democratic curriculum against the incorporation into passive participation. As Paulo Freire (1972, p. 56) pointed out:

> There is no such thing as a neutral educational process. Education either functions as an instrument that is used to facilitate the integration of the young into the logic of the present system and bring about conformity to it or it becomes the practice of freedom. [Education then becomes] then means by which men and women deal critically and creatively with reality and discover how to participate in the transformation of the world.

If communities are to become fully involved in democratic renewal maximum access to as much information as possible is needed, particularly research that will enable them to justify alternative views. Participatory action research is one way in which communities can build more systematic knowledge bases from their own experiences as counterweight to external, specialist knowledge. In addition, structures need to be in place to enable them to influence decision-making through developing their own ideas and agendas, pro-actively. They also need to have access to independent specialist advice that would enable them to develop their own policy analysis. All these issues are ones that the academy can make important contributions to as equal members of collaborative partnerships exchanging 'really useful knowledge' (Johnson, 1988, p. 22).

Knowledge and the Academy

The articulation of a vision that expresses the social nature of our experience, which aims to turn personal troubles into public issues and to support social movements that act to transform the world, are legitimate educational aims for the academy. However, university knowledge can easily become a commodity to be bought by those who have the necessary economic resources. To engage with civil society requires the reassertion of the social purpose tradition in education that sees students and other members of the community as 'knowledge subjects' (Freire, 1972) who bring intellectual, social and political resources with them. This means that rather than seeing knowledge as something that has to be accumulated and assessed through qualifications that signify our possession of it we should regard it a something we use, test, question and produce. Communities in civil society are often seen as needing knowledge that others possess. However, if rather than dichotomising the act of acquiring already existing knowledge from the activity of producing new knowledge we see instead that these two aspects of knowledge are dialectical, then we can transform these relations. As Jackson (1995, p.185) points out:

> *Adult bring something that derives both from their own experience of adult life and from their status as citizens to the educational process. Education [in the social purpose tradition] is based on a dialogue rather than a mere transmission of knowledge and skill; education is not only for personal development and advancement but also for social advancement; adult education constructs knowledge and not merely pass it on; adult education has a dialectical and organic relationships to social movements.*

From this perspective learning is essentially about making knowledge that makes sense of the world of those outside the gates of the academy in civil society and help them to act upon it collectively, in order to change it for the better. The curriculum always represents 'selections from a culture' (Williams, 1961) so knowledge is never really neutral or value free, and what counts as worth knowing reflects those particular social and political interests that have power to make it count. The tradition of social purpose education is not about rejecting the knowledge of the academy but rather is concerned to test this knowledge against the lived experience of its students and to harness the ways of understanding and acting that emerge from this process to a common and collective purpose. As Crowther, et al (2000, p. 173) point out:

> *The purpose is social in the sense that it is conceived in terms of the furthering the interests of exploited, oppressed and marginalised groups and it is part of their continuing struggle for greater democracy, social justice and equality.*

Change both in the academy and civil society towards greater equity will involve a radical rethinking of what counts as knowledge and understanding. Knowledge from this position would be actively constructed in the creative encounter between the expertise of the teacher and the experience of the students, with each role conferring a distinctive kind of authority. Educators have an important role in making sure that the complexity of the intellectual, emotional, practical, pleasurable and political possibilities of learning is not reduced to the apparent simplicity of targets, standards and skills (see Thompson, 2000). Finding a voice to do this can happen through being part of a social, mutually supportive group that is engaged in learning. Such learning is a political, as well as an educational, activity because spaces are opened up for the public discussion of issues with which people are concerned. Active groups can force into the public domain aspects of social conduct such as violence against women in the home that previously were discussed or were settled by traditional practices. This means that their voices, 'help to contest the traditional, the official, the patriarchal, the privileged and the academic view of things' (Thompson, 2000, p.143).

The emphasis on whose experiences count, and how they are interpreted and understood, helps us to challenge the 'common sense' of everyday assumptions about experience and its relationships to knowledge production. This allows new claims to be made for the legitimacy of reflexive experience leading to 'really useful knowledge' for those who are involved in generating it. In questioning the discourses that frame the ways of thinking, problems, and practices which are regarded as legitimate, it begins to be possible for people to open up new ways of reflexively thinking about the social construction of their experiences. When people create their own knowledge and have their voices heard, narrow definitions of what is thought to be 'educated knowledge' and who it is that makes it, are thrown into question. In this way the experiences and stories that have been excluded, and the mystifications caused by 'expert' knowledge, can be interrogated as a way of articulating views that come from below rather than above.

This is important because, in identifying and making space where alternative ways of thinking and being can be worked up, such practices increase the possibilities of knowledge – that is knowledge that is useful to those who generate it (Barr, 1999, p. 82).

Democratic Renewal and the Academy

There are a number of educational traditions in universities that make an important contribution to helping create a more just and democratic civil society. Scotland and Ireland both subscribe to the powerful myth that they are historically and culturally more democratic, egalitarian and open societies than England and that this kind of society should be demonstrated through egalitarian policies. It does not matter that this myth often masks an essentially meritocratic and highly gendered and 'raced' reality, because the 'social reality of the myth is always more potent than the empirical reality of the fact' (Martin, 1999, p. 3). One part of this cultural tradition in Scotland is the generalist tradition in higher education most cogently explored by George Davie in his book *The democratic intellect: Scotland and her universities in the nineteenth century* (1961). Davie points out the need for interdisciplinarity in educational practice and consequently the value of generalist rather than the specialist, and drew attention to the civic and educational power generated when one area of thought or expertise is illuminated by another. The generalist approach values the expert as part of the community but recognises that his or her value can only be realised if it is accepted that blind spots within the expert view are inevitable. Thus others within the community by virtue of their lack of expertise (which gives them a different perspective from that of the expert) have a responsibility to comment on these blind spots. The problems that this approach sought to address were those of over-specialisation and narrow focus on the technicalities of how to get things done. The case for the generalist tradition was the need to get to the root issues and causes of problems, in democratically informed ways, before questions of detail were addressed.

This tradition proves the basis for a distinctive vision of a rich and humane civic culture that is relevant and worth working for to-day. The argument Davie made for a democratic intellect in higher education, where non-specialists were encouraged to interrogate specialists, is a vital part of a healthy society and can equally be applied to adult and community education. The belief that an educated community of specialists are unfit to make decisions without processes of scrutiny leads to an understanding that they are, in effect, intellects without democracy. The issue for the educator is how to develop a curriculum that can facilitate the mutual illumination of blind spots in the sense referred to above. What is essential is to engage the critical intellect of people in a way that creates more rounded human beings and enables people to engage with public issues. Adult and community education is about the development of skills, human relationships and the engagement of people in understanding the wider social forces that impact both locally and globally. If people are to gain a voice they will need the confidence and authority that comes out of experience tempered by study, which provides opportunities for people to read meaning between the lines and the interests behind the meaning (see Crowther & Tett, 2001). For example, tackling racism requires the expertise of those who have directly suffered its effects as well as the general knowledge of those who seek to understand and counteract it. Understanding disability includes an awareness of the meaning of dependency, which becomes an educational resource both for disabled experts and interested generalists, rather than simply a technical problem to be solved. To live full lives people need an education that can equip them to develop their autonomy and control both at the individual and communal level. As Tawney (1926, p. 22) argued:

> If you want flowers you must have flowers, root and all, unless you are satisfied with flowers made of paper and tinsel. And if you want education you must have not cut it off from the social interests in which it has its living and perennial sources.

Redistribution and Recognition

How might this democratising tradition be used to promote greater equality through implementation of the current political interest in lifelong learning and social inclusion? There are always political choices to be made about the aims of development, and the state is not always clear about how its policies in these areas are to be implemented. These ambiguities at the heart of governmental policies lead to political and ethical choices for educators if they are to create a more equitable society. Such a society would involve both the redistribution of goods and services to those who currently lack them and the recognition of the cultural and social knowledge that people have. It would require adult and community educators to stimulate and support lifelong learning and reduce social exclusion through:

- exploring the contradictions of policy in ways that challenge discrimination and oppression;

- developing a curriculum that treats people as 'knowing subjects' and challenges them to take risks and develop further;

- helping people to recognise that they have the capacity to learn and to generate new, 'really useful' knowledge;

- working on both increasing skills and developing people's critical awareness of why they might not have these skills in the first place;

- using learning to build community capacity in civil society and increase individual and collective self-confidence.

Education can contribute to the extension of social democracy but this requires the valuing of difference as well as the need for shared understanding and agreement. The experiences of marginalized communities and their own definition of their needs are central to the organisation and delivery of appropriate learning and other services. People in civil society can be helped to develop their own forms of knowledge and so challenge the power of expert knowledge to monopolise the definition of what is wrong in their communities and what is needed to right it. This requires a democratising of the relationship between users and providers of services, both collectively and individually, and a sharing of the expert and lay knowledge. As Fiona Williams (1999, p. 684) argues:

> Solidarities need to be developed that are based on respect for difference: not the solidarity of the lowest common denominator, nor the solidarity that assumes that all will forgo their particularities in a common goal, rather it is the pursuit of unity in dialogues of difference. Such politics also has to involve both the redistribution of goods and the mutual recognition of worth.

This is a very demanding task for adult and community educators to help to achieve. However, if groups simply pursue the politics of recognition without addressing socio-economic inequalities, then they might win social justice for some in their group, but not for others. On the other hand the singular pursuit of issues of economic inequality can make invisible cultural injustices that render some groups, such as minority ethnic communities or marginalized young people, more vulnerable to economic exploitation.

An important role of the academy is to work with social movements which have always played an important part in stretching our imaginations about alternative ways of being because they open up questions about what we value and how we want to live. They ask questions about what type of society we want for the future and thus 'inject critique, vision and imagination into what we have learnt to take for granted' (Crowther, 1999, p. 36). By seeing the world as it is and how it might be, social movements are intrinsically utopian. In this sense utopia's proper role is to stir the imagination and challenge comfortable habits – a place to be desired rather than a place that does not exist. Adult and community educators too should be concerned with the world as it could be, as much as with the world as it is. This might be dismissed as cynical by the utopian, but without utopian thought our visions for the future are impoverished. It is important to begin questioning our desires and to test them against other desires in order to explore what is possible for the future. E.P. Thompson (1976, p. 790) commented, utopia's proper space is the education of desire in order 'to desire better, to desire more, and above all to desire in a different way.'

Conclusion: Fostering Autonomy

This paper has attempted to show that education can make an important contribution towards the building of more democratic, fairer society. However, there are powerful ideological and economic forces that seek to dominate, oppress and exploit people and 'the democratic state must learn how to foster the civic autonomy of communities – rather than seek, as often in the past, to co-opt and incorporate them' (Martin, 1999, p. 19). State policies in the areas of lifelong learning and social inclusion provide both problems and possibilities for helping to develop a clearer analysis of the nature of inequality and oppression. In order to do this, the knowledge and experiences of those that have been excluded need to be valued and the mystification caused by 'expert' knowledge requires to be interrogated. Having a greater say in education and learning is important, but being treated as capable citizens, with a right to dissent from provided solutions, is much more empowering and can lead to democratic renewal for all people. A popular curriculum that addresses the concerns of ordinary people and actively draws upon their experience as a resource for educational work increases the possibilities of developing knowledge that is useful to those who generate it. People then act both as experts regarding their own lives and as generalists too, commenting on others' blind spots about the root issues and causes of problems in civil society.

Approaching education and democratic renewal in this way may not be new but would involve revisiting much earlier debates over the role of education, as Margaret Davies argued in 1913:

> *Even a little knowledge is a dangerous thing. It causes a smouldering*
> *discontent, which may flame into active rebellion against a low level of life,*
> *and produces a demand, however stammering, for more interests and chances.*
> *Where we see ferment, there has been some of the yeast of education.*

(Quoted in Scott, 1998, p. 56)

If educators wish to see a fairer society then 'the yeast of education' will need to be applied to its work in civil society. This approach will be based on the notion of adult and community education as a *dissenting vocation* that takes the side of ordinary people against the ideological and economic forces that seek to dominate, oppress and exploit them (see Martin, 2001). Members of communities would then be perceived as active citizens making demands for change with their different ways of knowing and understanding the world being valued as a resource for learning. Rather than seeking to minimise risk, the academy should be 'educating desire' through challenging and supporting people in civil society to define and solve their problems for themselves.

References

Barr, J. (1999). Women, adult education and really useful knowledge. In J. Crowther, I. Martin & M. Shaw (Eds.), *Popular education and social movements in Scotland to-day* (pp. 70-82). Leicester: NIACE.

Beresford, P. & Croft, S. (1993). *Citizenship involvement: A practical guide for change.* London: Macmillan.

Crowther, J. (1999). Popular education and the struggle for democracy. In J. Crowther, I. Martin & M. Shaw (Eds.), *Popular education and social movements in Scotland to-day* (pp. 29-40). Leicester: NIACE.

Crowther, J., Martin, I. & Shaw, M. (2000). Turning the discourse. In J. Thompson (Ed.), *Stretching the academy.* Leicester: NIACE.

Crowther, J. & Tett, L. (2001). Democracy as a way of life: Literacy for citizenship. In J. Crowther, M. Hamilton & L. Tett (Eds.), *Powerful literacies* (pp. 108-118). Leicester NIACE.

Davie, G. (1961). *The democratic intellect: Scotland and her universities in the nineteenth century.* Edinburgh: Edinburgh University Press.

Freire, P. (1972). *Pedagogy of the oppressed.* Harmondsworth: Penguin.

Furedi, F. (1997). *A culture of fear: Risk-taking and the morality of low expectations.* London: Cassell.

Jackson, K. (1995). Popular education and the state: A new look at the community debate. In M. Mayo & J. Thompson (Eds.), *Adult Learning, critical intelligence and social change.* Leicester: NIACE.

Johnson, R. (1988). Really useful knowledge: 1790-1850. In T. Lovett, (Ed.), *Radical approaches to adult education: A reader.* London: Routledge.

Lister, R. (1997). Citizenship: Towards a feminist synthesis. *Feminist Review*, 57, 28-48.

Martin, I. (1999). Introductory essay: Popular education and social movements in Scotland today. In J. Crowther, I. Martin & M. Shaw (Eds.), *Popular education and social movements in Scotland to-day* (pp. 1-25). Leicester: NIACE.

Martin, I. (1999). What is lifelong learning for? Earning, yearning or yawning? *Adults Learning*, *13*(2), 14-17.

Scott, G. (1998). *Feminism and the politics of working women.* London: UCL Press.

Tawney, R.H. (1926). Adult education in the history of the nation. Paper read at the Fifth Annual Conference of the British Institute of Education.

Thompson, E.P. (1976). *William Morris.* New York: Pantheon Books.

Thompson, J. (2000). Life politics and popular learning. In J. Field & M. Leicester, (Eds.), *Lifelong learning: Education across the life-span* (pp. 134-145). London: Routledge.

Williams, F. (1999). Good enough principles for welfare. *Journal of Social Policy*, *28*(4), 667-687.

Williams, R. (1991). *The long revolution.* London: Pelican.

Picking Wild Orchids and Windflowers: Attachment Theory and Adult Education

TED FLEMING
NUI MAYNOOTH

Picking Wild Orchids and Windflowers: Attachment Theory and Adult Education

TED FLEMING
NUI MAYNOOTH

Introduction

In his *Memoirs* (2005) John McGahern tells of having survived a childhood of love and hatred in rural Ireland. He begins by talking about the 'inch deep' soil of Leitrim where one can trace 'the beaten path the otter takes between the lakes' and the 'quiet places on the edge of the lakes…where the otter feeds and trains her young' (p. 1). On the final page he returns to the otter, but also talks about his mother who died when he was eight:

> *She never really left us. In the worst years, I believe we would have been broken but for the different life we had known with her and the love she gave that was there like hidden strength.*
>
> *When I reflect on those rare moments when I stumble without warning into that extraordinary sense of security, that deep peace, I know that consciously and unconsciously she has been with me all my life.*
>
> *If we could walk together through those summer lanes, with their banks of wild flowers that 'cast a spell', we probably would not be able to speak, though I would want to tell her all the local news.*
>
> *We would leave the lanes and I would take her by the beaten path the otter takes under the thick hedges between the lakes. At the lake's edge I would show her the green lawns speckled with fish bones and blue crayfish shells where the otter feeds and trains her young…*
>
> *As we retraced our steps, I would pick for her the wild orchid and the windflower.*
>
> (McGahern, 2005, pp. 271-272)

McGahern knew that his mother forged for him a secure childhood and he carried this security with him all his life. This paper will explore the nature of this security and the implications for adult learning.

Adult education has grown accustomed to a particular palette of debates involving lifelong learning and a more critical understanding of learning. However, neo-liberal and functionalist educators have colonized the lifelong learning debate with a fixation on technique, the economy and vocationalism (Welton, 1995). There are exceptions (Murphy,

2001) but even when the debate turns to more critical perspectives, as in Brookfield's work on critical theory (2005), there is a missing dimension. Tennant's (2006) psychology textbook omits ideas that have a biological base. We do not have a predisposition in adult education to explore ideas that are introduced with the words: 'Consider the performance of the long-tailed tit...' (Bowlby, 1979, p. 28). But a palette of ideas bounded by a resistance to critical theory on the one hand and on the other by a resistance to looking at a biological base for human actions is a very narrow palate indeed.

This paper aims to address this lacuna and illustrate how attachment theory is of profound and neglected importance for a comprehensive understanding of adult development and learning. The importance of these ideas for adult learning was first prompted by work my wife has being doing on attachment theory (Neville, 2000).

Bowlby's theory of attachment is based on a number of understandings. First, children in orphanages, who suffered from maternal deprivation, the absence of fathers, siblings and a family environment, were liable to cognitive and affective consequences. Second, the developmental importance for animals of the early contact between mother and infant is established (Bowlby, 1969, pp. 184-190). The image of Konrad Lorenz (Bowlby, 1969, p. 210) being followed by a line of goslings comes to mind. Subsequent experiments on rhesus monkeys with wire framed models as parents showed that young monkeys developed abnormal social behaviours including being abusive towards their own offspring. It is these images that may have led to the neglect of these ideas.

John Bowlby

John Bowlby's (1907-1991) work with children from poor backgrounds convinced him that family life was important for their emotional development. In 1944 at the London Child Guidance Clinic (where he worked with Melanie Klein) he found that there was a connection between the behaviour of thieving children and their experiences in chaotic families without a consistent caregiver (Bowlby, 1944). He found that separation of infant from mother was detrimental to the infant's development.

In post-war Britain, at the Tavistock Clinic, in collaboration with James and Joyce Robertson, he studied the effects of separation on children. Their short film (Robertson & Robertson, 1953) about a secure well-adjusted child placed temporarily in care and the suffering endured still leaves an impact on the viewer. The film documents the distress and disintegration of the child who experiences maternal deprivation as a deeply traumatic event. The film changed the way hospitals involved parents in the care of children. From then:

early separations are recognised as inherently dangerous for children; the mourning process is accepted as necessary rather than self-indulgent. But his greatest influence is where we would wish it to be, on the social arrangements that are made for children…in hospitals, in nursery schools, in care and…at home.

(Gomez, 1997, p. 53)

In trying to understand the causes of delinquency (Bowlby, 1944), the nature of the child's ties to mother (Bowlby, 1958), the meaning of separation anxiety (Bowlby, 1960a) and the significance of grief and mourning for young children (Bowlby, 1960b), he began to devise theories that were outlined in three books: *Attachment and Loss* (1969); *Separation: Anxiety and Anger* (1973) and *Loss: Sadness and Depression* (1980). A strong social concern runs through his work and he saw the emotional deprivation of children as a social ill, distorting and degrading the fabric of social life (Bowlby, 1953). He supported:

Training cadres of child-care workers and psychotherapists who are sensitive to the emotional needs of children and their parents; helping people to find security in their lives through the fostering of close emotional bonds;… In these ways the vicious circles of deprivation can be broken, this generation's insecure young people no longer condemned to reproduce their own insecurities in the next.

These attitudes permeate almost every paragraph Bowlby wrote…

(Holmes, 1993 p. 201)

Bowlby reached the conclusion that aggression sprung from insecure attachments and in the absence of care the seeds of destruction and rage are sown (Holmes, 1993, p. 204). Disadvantage and poverty have psychological implications.

Bowlby on Attachment Theory

It is unlikely that infants will survive without the care of an adult and there are inbuilt biological and evolutionary based predispositions in both adults and infants that contribute to the survival and development of the child (Bowlby, 1979, p. 37). Infants are 'programmed' to seek and precipitate appropriate adult reactions so that their survival and developmental needs are met. When left alone for even a short time or when cold, hungry or uncomfortable the child expresses distress in such a way as to make it both normal to want to respond and satisfying to attend to that distress. In this way infants are not passive recipients of care, but innately proactive in constructing caring relationships. This attachment dance is the trigger for attachment behaviours in the parent. Attachment behaviour is:

Any form of behaviour that results in a person attaining or retaining proximity to some other differentiated and preferred individual, who is usually conceived as stronger and/or wiser.

(Bowlby, 1979, p. 129)

The protective and comforting behaviour of the carer provides a secure base for the infant and interactions involving play, baby talk, making close eye contact, playing with objects and the excitement of the engagements are the initial ventures into the world for the child (Bowlby, 1969, p. 304). For Bowlby, parenting involves providing appropriate responses to the child's need for security (Bowlby, 1979, p. 136). About one in three children grow up without this experience (Bowlby, 1979, p. 136).

Attachment is the 'process whereby infants and young children develop deep confidence in their parents' protection' and this enduring tie provides security (Goldberg, 2000, p. 8). The child's experience of attachment strongly influences subsequent reactions to stress, to relationships, self-esteem, sense of security and identity. If a parent is not available through neglect, illness or inattention this is likely to result in insecure attachment. Although the first attachment is almost always to the mother Bowlby's theory applies to and holds for any primary carer whether male or female, parent or carer. Bowlby observed that the child's attachment figure appeared to provide a secure base (a developmental platform) from which the infant could safely explore their environment and to which they could return if tired, stressed or in perceived danger or need (Bowlby, 1988, p. 11). It is not until the child is about three that they can begin to tolerate separation and keep alive a sense that the caregiver, though absent, is still available.

Mary Ainsworth made significant contributions to the theory and studied the stress resulting from separation of child and mother (the strange situation) with an emphasis on the importance of a secure base provided by the mother (Ainsworth, et al., 1978).

Secure and Insecure Attachments

Generally, when children have introjected their experiences of being cared for they will have a model of both themselves as valued and of key others as validating, responsive and predictable. As a result they will have a greater sense of 'felt security', more effective strategies for getting help when they need it and more optimistic views of social relationships. Such children are securely attached (Bowlby, 1969, p. 339). Infants who are **securely attached** are happy to explore their environment. When the mother leaves they continue to explore but in a slightly diminished way. When mother returns, though they might or might not cry, they greet her positively and are easily comforted. Research continues (Howe, 1995a, 1995b) and:

> ...there is a strong case for believing that an unthinking confidence in the unfailing accessibility and support of attachment figures is the bedrock on which stable and self-reliant personality is built.

(Bowlby, 1973, p. 366)

The mother of a secure child has achieved this by being sensitive and appropriately responsive to the child's needs for security, and by being able to construct for the child an experience of being cared for. Such a mother may be characterised as psychologically available to the child, emotionally expressive and flexible in dealing with babies.

> *The family experience of those who grow up to become relatively stable*
> *and self-reliant is characterized not only by unfailing parental support when*
> *called upon but also by a steady yet timely encouragement towards increasing*
> *autonomy, and by the frank communication by parents of working models –*
> *of themselves, of child, and of others – that are not only tolerably valid but*
> *open to be questioned and revised.*

(Bowlby, 1973, p. 367)

More recent research has developed the concept of 'mind-mindedness' to describe the ability of a parent to understand and respond not only to the infant's feelings but also to their thinking (Meins, et al., 2002). The secure individual is inclined to be optimistic about coping, more likely to relate better to others, have greater capacity for concentration and cooperation and be more confident and resilient. They can express emotions openly and appropriately, acknowledge the physiological signs of anger, can control anger and have better mental health and relationships (Belsky, 2002).

In addition to secure attachments there are insecure attachments that have been categorised as avoidant, anxious and disorganised. These attachments are defensive strategies that attempt to maintain contact with rejecting or inconsistent parents.

The **avoidant attached** child is usually unconcerned with either the presence or the absence of the mother and does not express attachment needs so as to avoid the risk of rejection. They can be more friendly with strangers than with the carer. The primary carer may not reject the child but may exhibit low levels of response to the distress of the child who is encouraged to get on with life and not make too many demands. The mother may be uncomfortable with close contact or have feelings of resentment or may be slow responding to distress or minimally expressive or relatively rigid in dealing with infants.

The **anxious/ambivalent attached** child (Bowlby, 1969, p. 338, 1973, p. 245, 1979, p. 137; Ainsworth, et al., 1978) is usually preoccupied with getting attention. The mother in this case is more likely to be inconsistent, insensitive to signals from the child or inept at engaging in physical contact and show little spontaneous affection. The child is preoccupied with the mother and is reluctant to explore even in her presence. The departure of the mother increases distress significantly. Comforting responses are resisted, rejected or ignored. This child has a picture of themselves as not lovable, not worthy of care, and of their parents as having to be manipulated into caring (Gomez, 1997, p. 161).

Finally, the **disorganised** attachment style was discovered by Main and Solomon (1986) and is associated with consistently inadequate care, maltreatment or depressed carer. The cause may be unresolved attachment loss or trauma in the early experience of the parent (Main & Hess, 1990).

Strange situation

Mary Ainsworth studied what happens to a child when their parent leaves the room or a stranger approaches. In this **strange situation** the child may experience separation anxiety. This situation is used as an analytical tool to assess attachment style, to assess the quality of early attachments and the nature of the mother-baby relationship.

Internal working models

Attachment operates by each child developing an internal representation of their experiences of the world of relationships that develops into what Bowlby called an internal working model of social relating (Bowlby, 1969, p. 80, 1973, p. 237). Infants, children and adults, base their understanding of social behaviour on these models. The internal working model implies that it is just that, a model like an architect's model, of how the individual perceives the world of relationships to be. Models guide social interactions and inform understandings of other people.

A securely attached child (or adult) will have internal working models that make meaning of the world as a safe place and of themselves as responsive, caring, reliable and a self that is worthy of love and attention. They will bring this way of making sense of relationships to all their relationships. On the other hand, an insecurely attached child (or adult) may view the world as a dangerous place in which other people are to be treated with caution and will see themselves as not worthy of attention and love (Holmes, 1993, p. 79).

Biological base of attachments

While the bonds between parents and infants are shaped by personal experience the basic impetus for the formation of internal working models is biological. A number of researchers have built on the work of Bowlby and have been able to demonstrate that infants and children deprived of affective bonding and human contact (Romanian orphanages) have gaps in the part of their brains that deals with relationships (Schore, 1994, 2001). Going further, they demonstrate that parts of the brain that deal with relationships are constructed in the early years of life in response to the actions of parents. Their actions through play, talking and communicating trigger the physical development of the brain and the way it is 'wired.' Our brain is constructed as it grows in response to interpersonal stimulation. If attachment stimulation is absent, that part of the brain is not developed.

Adult Attachment

Attachment behaviour characterises humans from the cradle to the grave and becomes evident when adults are under stress, become ill, afraid or in emergencies (Bowlby, 1979, p. 129, 1988 p. 27). Patterns established in childhood endure into adulthood and tend to structure the way we interact and relate. Attachment style and behaviours persist through life (Bowlby, 1988, p. 126) and undergo developmental transformation. Adult attachments are linked to one's own childhood during which internal working models were constructed and in turn influence one's own parenting behaviour and ability to create secure attachments. This intergenerational dimension is important.

Internal working models can be revised in the light of experience, but they are not always or indeed easily accessible to conscious examination and change, because they were laid down early in the child's development (Bowlby, 1973, p. 367). The attachment orientations of care givers (adults) influence their attachments with their infants and children and the parent's attachment style is in this way transmitted across the generations (Bowlby, 1969, p. 348).

Bowlby saw that:

> *Whatever representational models of attachment figures and of self an individual builds up during childhood and adolescence, tend to persist relatively unchanged into and throughout life. As a result he tends to assimilate any new person with whom he may form a bond, such as a spouse or child, or employer or therapist, to an existing model...and may continue to do so despite repeated evidence that the model is inappropriate.*
>
> *Such biased perceptions and expectations lead to various misconceived beliefs about the other people, to false expectations about the way they will behave and to inappropriate actions, intended to forestall their expected behaviour.*
>
> (Bowlby, 1979, p. 142)

Attachment not only influences our ability to love but also to work. Hazan and Shaver (1990) assert that adult attachment supports work in the same way that infant attachment supports exploration and that the healthy balance between attachment and exploration in the infant is similar to the love/work balance in adulthood.

Attachment and Adult Learning

Attachment theory has a number of implications for adult education. These include the importance of:

- attachment styles and internal working models;

- the strange situation;

- attachment theory for transformative learning.

Attachment styles and internal working models

Bowlby envisages the role of the therapist as providing the conditions in which a patient can explore their representational models of themselves and their attachment figures with a view to reappraising and restructuring them in the light of the new understandings acquired and the new experiences one has in the therapeutic relationship (Bowlby, 1988, p. 138). He goes on to describe the role of the therapist as providing the patient with a secure base from which the past may be explored. Therapy involves assisting the patient to explore the ways he/she now engages in relations with significant others and what unconscious biases there may be in one's close or intimate relationships. The therapist encourages the patient to explore how the current situation is an expression of how one's own experiences in childhood may continue to impact on current relationships and helps in recognising that the models the patient has of themselves and their relationships may or may not be appropriate to the present or future, or indeed may not have been justified at all (Bowlby, 1988, p. 138). In this way 'one may cease to be a slave to old and unconscious stereotypes and to feel, think and to act in new ways' (Bowlby, 1988, p. 139). This is an appropriate agenda for many adult education courses and programmes in personal development.

In working with students the teacher too will think, feel, act and have expectations based on their own internal working models that act as basic assumptions. These working models will influence the educator's reactions to learners who in turn are secure or otherwise. I am suggesting that in the training of adult educators it is worth increasing awareness of the ways one's own internal working models and attachment styles lead one to understand or misunderstand the interpersonal communications of others, particularly students.

Thus the adult educator could see themselves as both aware of how they as tutor may be construing the world out of their attachment styles and internal working models as well as providing opportunities for learners to reconstruct and develop their own attachment styles and models.

Internal working models in adults affect our cognitive, emotional and behavioural responses to others in family, work and in all communications. They affect how data is evaluated and experienced, accepted, rejected or ignored, how communications are interpreted and responded to, how we evaluate others. Cognitive responses may lead to giving selective attention to others; to biases in memory; and impact on our inferences and explanations. Emotional response patterns and behaviour are also influenced by internal working models. In any activity that involves thinking, the question arises as to how one's internal working models influence that thinking? The thoughts we have, what we remember, what we consider important, how we interpret and make sense of events, are influenced by these models. Secure adults are more likely to integrate the cognitive and emotional and are less likely to be dominated by one or the other. But those with anxious attachments will focus on the emotional rather than the cognitive and those with avoidant style will overly rely on the cognitive factors and ignore or deny emotional reactions such as anxiety or fear (Feeney & Noller, 1996, p. 105). Attachment theory in this way helps us elaborate on what is more traditionally known as learning styles (Tennant, 2006, p. 86).

The recently developed concept of 'mind-mindedness' encourages and gives a developmental rationale for parents to focus on the feelings and thinking process of the child. There is a predictive link between maternal mind-mindedness and secure attachments (Mein, et al., 2002, p. 1717). Though this idea is not yet sufficiently researched, there is the tantalising possibility that the tutor who is capable of understanding both the feelings and thinking process of the learner will have the developmental dividend of a secure environment for learning and development.

Strange situation

The strange situation is a technique for identifying one's attachment style. Adult education provides strange situations for students. For example, when a student joins a course for the first time, or when confronted with new ideas, these are strange situations. In adult education we come across and precipitate such strange situations or experiences that perplex, disorient, or make the learner curious. What happens, if we accept the insights of Bowlby, is most interesting. These situations induce a sense of loss. Meanings that were taken for granted as true become open for discussion, debate, examination, scrutiny and change. Students make meaning of the strange situations in ways that are consistent with their internal working models. Whether they are secure or insecure, this will impact on their feelings and attitudes, and how they interpret and act in these situations. The adult educator who produces a strange situation has the ethical responsibility to provide a safe space for exploring new ideas and situations. Of course, one's ability to do this is provocatively in proportion to the tutor's secure or insecure attachment styles and internal working models. The logic of the strange situation is what I imagine Maxine Greene means when she talks about the 'teacher as stranger' (Greene, 1973).

Transformation Theory

Transformation theory is the understanding of adult learning developed by Mezirow (1996). Internal working models are epistemic meaning schemes and in transformation theory it is such meaning schemes, these frames of reference that get transformed (Mezirow, 1996, p. 7). One dimension of transformative learning involves the process of developing new internal working models. It is also consistent with attachment theory to see the creation of perplexity as a way of prompting transformative learning which call this perplexity a disorienting dilemma. In addition, we can come to understand how a new working model may be an improvement on a previous one by applying the criteria (from transformation theory) of being more inclusive, more discriminating and more open to future change as the criteria for judging an improved internal working model.

As one's attachment style informs ways of relating to others it is suggested here that a significant kind of adult learning involves the transformative and developmental task of moving toward more secure attachments and the new identity implied by this. This adds an important aim for adult development that ranks with the pathways outlined by Erikson, Kohlberg and Gilligan.

In transformative learning theory a key role is given to meaning as the organisation of experience. We order experiences, relate them to previous experiences and use them to make decisions about how to act in the future. This organisation of experience allows us order and classify events and recognise feelings associated with events. By perceiving experience as having a pattern that is recognisable we can learn (Marris, 1991, p. 78). The process of growing up is at least partly the process of developing these organisations of meaning. The activity of adult learning involves the process of changing these organisations of meaning. But transformative learning theory adds a critical dimension by emphasising how these organisations of meaning are transformed by critical reflection on assumptions.

Both attachment theory and transformation theory are equally interested in the loss of meaning resulting from change in one's environment. In both theories it is acknowledged that loss, such as the death of a partner, child or friend may raise unnerving questions for our central meaning making system. In attachment theory there is an interest in the way one's attachment style and internal working models will impact on the experience of grief while in transformation theory there is an emphasis on the way meaning schemes produce understandings that are adequate or not for interpreting the current situation. Meanings break down not only because new events may not be capable of being explained by the current meanings but also because the purposes that informed the current ordering may get disrupted. Contradictions, incompatibilities, inconsistencies, anomalies, become clear, emerge and are heightened by changing circumstances. This tendency is an uncertainty that parallels Mezirow's disorienting dilemma. Our meanings are not secure or fixed and in many situations uncertainty flings itself on us.

In adult education that so often engages in sharing experiences, telling stories and learning from each other, these ideas are particularly important. What we perceive, the stories we tell and the coherence with which we tell them and our reactions to our own and other's stories is based on our own internal working models.

Human development is being redefined here as the transformation of attachment styles and internal working models and as previously suggested involves the transformation of attachment narratives (Fleming, 2003).

Critique

Neither the work of Bowlby nor Ainsworth was readily accepted by developmental psychologists. Rutter (1997) provided a series of structured critical reviews of attachment theory.

One of the main criticisms of attachment theory concerns the idea that infant experiences determine adult behaviour. Research confirms that there is considerable scope for later change in attachment style but also points to a strong link between child and adult attachment. The word 'determine' is not optimal but early experiences make a unique contribution to adulthood. Change is always possible but is constrained by previous adaptations (Goldberger, 2000, p. 247).

Attachment theory is seen as unfairly blaming the mother who is in many cases the primary care-giver. No amount of political correctness will disguise the reality that it is most often the mother who is the main attachment figure and what she does and how she reproduces attachment styles is a crucial factor in how a child develops. But so often the resources that some mothers bring to parenting compromise the attachments they would like to forge. Even the idea that a child may spend considerable hours in childcare or crèche facilities compounds the guilt of parents and especially mothers. The dilemma for parents is how to balance the needs of the child for secure attachments with increasing social and economic demands for women to work. The challenge is to navigate the complex and difficult issues without increasing guilt or perceiving blame.

Bowlby raises the human trauma of maternal deprivation above all other trauma. Fathers are rarely looked at and have no intrinsic value at all. All possible shades of experience are reduced to one or other variety of attachment pattern. Little is known about how internal working models are constructed or how later in childhood or adulthood, they are reconstructed, transformed. We cannot look at internal working models directly, and so must make inferences from their output, e.g. drawings, narratives and behaviour, etc. More work needs to be done on these constructs.

The work of Bowlby was undertaken in the shadow of the WW2 where huge amounts of separation were experienced by men and women. However, he rarely explores these experiences where, in particular, women were left to rear children and earn a living in the absence of a husband and father for the children. The resulting distress caused to men and women is not explored at all.

One could also make the argument that the emphasis in Bowlby on maternal deprivation is a reflection of post-war England where many children were shocked by the separations of war. Bowlby was a welcome reemphasis of the values of mothering. In addition, it could be argued that in emphasising the role of mothers providing individual care for children he let the state or government off the hook – they should have been doing more to provide child care.

Feminists object that Bowlby is using biology to justify what is essentially a cultural product of our own 'patriarchal but father-absent' society (Holmes, 1993, p. 47). This division of labour fits modern society, leaving men free and women fettered. It can also be argued that in Bowlby the nature and nurture debate is given an interpretation that emphasises the interaction between them – nature and nurture.

These critiques lead us to see that attachment theory, like all theory is contested, partial and always in need or development.

Conclusion

We are coming to terms slowly and painfully with the way we have reared children in Ireland. Tribunal and inquiries investigate child abuse and violence towards children in both the church and in state run child care institutions. The record on taking care of children, particularly when they were born outside marriage, is not good and too many children are in search of parents they never knew and parents in search of children they gave up for adoption.

There is a high correlation between the attachment behaviour of the carer and the resulting attachment characteristics of the child.

The experience of attachment is the first crucial link between sociological and psychological understanding: the experience of attachment, which so profoundly influences the growth of personality, is itself the product of a culture, and a determinant of how that culture will be reproduced in the next generation – not only the culture of attachment itself but all our ideas of order, authority, and control (Marris, 1991, pp. 79-80).

It is for these reasons that I am drawn to McGahern and his *Memoirs*. There the drama is narrated in cruel detail about his father but also the stories of a life sustaining attachment with his mother. I think he must have known, or come to some understanding about, the ability of good parenting to carry a person through life.

I am also reminded of Toni Morrison's *The Bluest Eye* where Claudia is explaining how she hates Shirley Temple dolls that are a representation of the world of things to be possessed and a reminder of how white dolls are given as presents to black children. She destroyed these dolls:

*...nobody ever asked me what I wanted for Christmas. Had any adult with the
power to fulfil my desires taken me seriously and asked me what I wanted, they
would have known that I did not want to have anything to own, or to possess
any object. I wanted to feel something on Christmas day. The real question
would have been 'Dear Claudia, what experience would you like on Christmas?'
I could have spoken up, 'I wanted to sit on a low stool in Big Mama's kitchen
with my lap full of lilacs and listen to Big Papa play his violin for me alone.'
The lowness of the stool made for my body, the security and warmth of
Big Mama's kitchen, the smell of the lilacs, the sound of music, and, since
it would be good to have all of my senses engaged, the taste of peach,
perhaps, afterwards.*

(Morrison, 1990, p. 15)

In these ways we develop secure attachments, and as a consequence are able to
construct such attachments for our children, and to facilitate growth in our own adult
attachment styles.

References

Ainsworth, M.D.S., Blehar, M.C., Waters, E. & Wall, S. (1978). *Patterns of attachment.*
Hillsdale NJ: Lawrence Erlbaum.

Belsky, J. (2002). Developmental origins of attachment styles. *Attachment and Human
Development, 4*(2), 166-170.

Bowlby, J. (1944). Forty-four juvenile thieves: Their characters and home lives. *International
Journal of Psychoanalysis, 25*, 19-52.

Bowlby, J. (1953). *Childcare and the growth of maternal love.* Harmondsworth: Penguin.

Bowlby, J. (1958). The nature of the child's tie to his mother. *International Journal of
Psychoanalysis, 39*, 350-373.

Bowlby, J. (1960a). Separation anxiety. *International Journal of Psychoanalysis, 41*,
89-113.

Bowlby, J. (1960b). Grief and mourning in infancy and early childhood. *The Psychoanalytic
Study of the Child, 15*, 9-52.

Bowlby, J. (1969). *Attachment and Loss Vol 1: Attachment.* New York: Basic Books.

Bowlby, J. (1973). *Attachment and Loss Vol 2: Separation, anxiety and anger.* New York:
Basic Books.

Bowlby, J. (1979). *The making and breaking of affectional bonds.* London: Tavistock.

Bowlby, J. (1980). *Attachment and Loss, Vol 3: Loss, sadness and depression.* New York: Basic Books.

Bowlby, J. (1988). *A secure base: Clinical applications of attachment theory.* London: Routledge.

Brookfield, S. (2005). *The power of critical theory: Liberating adult learning and teaching.* San Francisco: Jossey-Bass.

Feeney, J. & Noller, P. (1996). *Adult attachment.* London: Sage.

Fleming, T. (2003). Narrative means to transformative ends: Towards a narrative language for Transformation. In C.A. Wiessner, S.R. Meyer, N.L. Pfhal, & P.G. Neaman (Eds.), *Transformative learning in action: Building bridges across contexts and disciplines,* (pp. 179-184). New York: Columbia University.

Goldberg, S. (2000). *Attachment and development.* London: Arnold.

Gomez, L. (1997). *An introduction to object relations.* London: Free Association Press.

Greene, M. (1973). *Teacher as stranger: Educational philosophy for the modern age.* Belmont, CA: Wadsworth.

Hazan, C. & Shaver, P.R. (1990). Love and work: An attachment-theoretical perspective. *Journal of Personality and Social Psychology, 59*(2), 270-280.

Holmes, J. (1993). *John Bowlby and attachment theory.* London: Routledge.

Howe, D. (1995a). Adoption and attachment. *Adoption and Fostering,* 19(4), 7-15.

Howe, D. (1995b). *Attachment theory for social work practice.* London: Macmillan Press.

McGahern, J. (2005). *Memoirs.* London: Faber & Faber.

Main, M. & Hess, E. (1990). Parents' unresolved traumatic experiences are related to infant disorganised attachment status: Is frightened and/or frightening behaviour the linking mechanism? In M.T. Greenberg, D. Ciccetti, & E.M. Cummins (Eds.), *Attachment in the preschool years* (pp. 161-184). Chicago, IL: University of Chicago Press.

Main, M. & Solomon, J. (1986). Discovery of a new, insecure-disorganised/disoriented attachment pattern. In T. Brazelton & M. Youngman, (Eds.), *Affective development in infancy* (pp. 95-124). Norwood, NJ: Ablex.

Marris, P. (1991). The social construction of uncertainty. In Parkes, et al., *Attachment across the Lifecycle* (pp. 77-92). London: Routledge.

Meins, E., Ferynhough, C., Wainwright, R., Gupta, M.D., Fradley, E. & Tuckey, M. (2002). Maternal mind-mindedness and attachment security as predictors of theory of mind understanding. *Child Development*, *73*(6), 1715-1726.

Mezirow, J. (1996). Adult education and empowerment for individual and community development. In B. Connolly, T. Fleming, A. Ryan & D. McCormack (Eds.), *Radical learning for liberation* (pp. 5-13). Maynooth: MACE.

Morrison, T. (1990). *The bluest eye.* London: Picador.

Murphy, M. (2001). Adult education, lifelong learning and the end of political economy. *Studies in the Education of Adults*, *32*(2), 166-181.

Neville, P. (2000). Assessments for inter-country adoption in the North-Eastern Health Board: A search for a new model. Unpublished MA Thesis, National University of Ireland, Dublin.

Roberston, J. & Robertson, J. (1953). *John* [Film]. University Park. PA: Pennsylvania State Audio Visual Services.

Rutter, M. (1997). Clinical implications of attachment concepts: Retrospect and prospect. In A. Schore, (1994). *Affect regulation and the origin of self.* Hove: Lawrence Erlbaum.

Schore, A. (2001). Effects of a secure attachment, relationship of right brain development. affect regulation and infant mental health. *Infant Mental Health Journal*, *22*(1-2), 7-66.

Tennant, M. (2006). *Psychology and adult learning* (3rd ed.). London: Routledge.

Welton, M. (Ed.). (1995). *In defense of the lifeworld: Critical perspectives on adult learning.* New York: SUNY.

Demanding Reflexivity:
Lazy Ozzie and Other Stories

DAVID McCORMACK
NUI MAYNOOTH

Demanding Reflexivity: Lazy Ozzie and Other Stories

DAVID McCORMACK
NUI MAYNOOTH

Introduction

I am a staff member in a University Department of Adult and Community Education, which espouses rather grandly, a radical approach to adult education theory, practice and research. I think of how two researchers in the Department recently articulated this approach. 'The goal of radical adult education' according to one is 'to transform unjust structures and systems in society through collective action for social change' (McGlynn, 2006, p. 36). Radical adult education, he says echoing Marx, 'is emancipatory because it is not sufficient to explain the world, it is also necessary to act to change it' (McGlynn, 2006, p. 37). The other researcher sees individual agency as an important aspect of critical and collective social action, particularly in addressing hegemonic discourses that both structure our subjectivities and identities and perpetuate inequalities (Kenny, 2006, pp. 22-24, 26-7).

I always feel inadequate in the face of these weighty pronouncements. But I increasingly suspect that I am not alone in feeling that personal and social change are much more complex matters than we ordinarily admit and that research adds another element of complexity, and that supervising research yet another. I think it is true and fair to say that supervising research in this field raises ethical issues of various kinds, not least in relation to the well being of the supervisee. It also raises issues of the kind of relationship that the supervisor sets up with the supervisee: tending as it often does to issues of the transformative learning of the researcher.

One of the orthodoxies of supervising research within the framework of a radical approach to adult education is that you 'demand' a reflexive approach. That is, you ask that the researcher adopt a paradigm of research that does not pretend scientific validity, one that recognises that the researcher's own assumptions, experiences and subjectivity constitute the major source of colour in the canvas he or she is painting. Reflexivity in research involves developing 'critical literacy' by not only exploring the external world but also turning the research gaze both on the medium of research and on the researcher him/herself (Davies et al., 2006, p. 88). Researchers therefore, as well as being concerned with doing research, are also concerned with their own story as researchers and with the story of the research.

But the layers are often complex and troubling. As Davies and colleagues recognise (2006) writing and researching reflexively is a fraught process. So reflexivity as a key aspect of research in adult education is both demanded (by the discipline) and demanding (of the researcher). This paper is a story about both of those processes and the complex dynamic that reflexivity sets up.

The Elusive Self

'My own study has become part of my everyday life, and I wonder will my data collection ever cease', says St. Pierre (1997) and I know the feeling. Except, I would put it the other way around, my everyday life has become part of my study and the thread of what I want to say is as elusive as the self in Zagajewski's poem:

> It is small and no more visible than a cricket
> in August. It likes to dress up, to masquerade,
> as all dwarfs do. It lodges between
> granite blocks, between serviceable
> truths. It even fits under
> a bandage, under adhesive.

(Zagajewski, 2004, p. 31)

At this point I am tired pursuing the thread, the heart of the matter, and it has slipped into the cracks and crevices of the numerous drafts I have done. The fact that the search is for something of little consequence to anyone save me, and takes place in the detritus of the mundane doesn't matter. This straightforward task of writing a paper has been, in a way, shattering, so bear with me as I try to put one foot in front of the other and tell you the story of writing a story.

I wrote *Lazy Ozzie* months ago. A short story written at one sitting after a tense day ruminating over a meeting with a research student. I kind of liked it, felt better for writing it and felt it captured some of the intimate flux of the meeting and its aftertaste. I felt I had done what Ellis and Bochner suggest that personal narratives can do:

> *[they] create the effect of reality, showing characters embedded in the*
> *complexities of lived moments of struggle, resisting the intrusions of chaos,*
> *disconnection, fragmentation, marginalization, and incoherence, trying to*
> *preserve or restore the continuity and coherence of life's unity in the face of*
> *unexpected blows of fate that call one's meanings and values into question.*

(Ellis and Bochner, 2000, p. 744)

Even though I can't bear to read it anymore, and hate and detest it more with every draft of this paper that I write, *Lazy Ozzie* is part of the story and so I offer it here as a part of the story I want to tell.

Lazy Ozzie[3]

Unhinged with tiredness and strange to myself as a familiar word repeated, I wait for Janice. She arrives and we have a stern supervisory meeting. 'You are getting mixed up', I tell her. 'You can't do a thesis without having a clear sense of what it is you want to find out and how you want to find it out.' I speak with the authority of a supervisor of long standing. I know how to structure arguments and she just isn't doing the business.

But that's not all. A creeping voice asks me is it me. Am I making the mess? Do I understand research well enough?

'I just don't know if you are going to make the deadline at this rate. Have you thought of deferral as an option? Last year John just needed two extra weeks and he did really well, got his first.'

'You wouldn't be a perfectionist by any chance?' she asks. I answer quickly for fear of smarting and getting angry. 'It isn't about my perfectionism, this is about something being good enough.' I should know better, hang back a bit, quell the retaliatory impulse, let the question wash over me a bit.

I tell her that there are at least two selves at play: the practitioner self and the researcher self. We draw them on the page and all the other selves around them: the supervisor, the group, the course organisers… 'You need to be clear that you think differently when you are a group facilitator and when you are a researcher. You need to ask the questions that the researcher would ask.'

The session ends. Another session follows and ends in which I say many of the same things. I am drained going home and ruminate all the way, passing hedges and people in a blear of preoccupation.

At home Martha and Ellen want a story. I find one we have never read before about Lazy Ozzie. Lazy Ozzie is an owl that just wanted to be wise but didn't want to learn how to fly. I wake up a little. I want to be wise but have often very little evidence of it, am not really interested in the blear eyed learning that gains real wisdom. Janice has really gotten into me. Undermined me. But she doesn't want to fly either. She wants to be a researcher but doesn't want to learn the craft. I'm supposed to tell her what to do.

---

3   The Children's story referred to is Coleman, M. and Williamson, G. *Lazy Ozzie*, London, Little Tiger Press.

Ozzie's mom goes off one day. 'Now Ozzie when I come back I want you to be on the ground and then I will know you have flown.' My interest is piqued, though Martha and Ellen are not too interested. Ozzie has a great idea. He calls over the horse and convinces him to let him down on his back and to take him to the cow. He convinces her to take him to the pig. Martha is no longer sitting down. 'Want go ming' she says. The ming is the swing but that's not what she means, she actually wants the slide. I am as dislocated as an unfinished sentence. I put her on to the slide, seat her at the top and whee down she goes. 'Gain. Gain. Daddy.' I put her on to the slide, seat her at the top and whee down she goes. 'Gain. Gain. Daddy.' I put her up, place her at the top, talk to her about what I am doing and down she goes. I put her up, place her at the top, all the while intrigued with Ozzie. How will the story end? The parallels with Janice are so striking. She wants to fly but is finding ways of avoiding it. Am I the horse, I wonder, giving her a hand down?

I put Martha up on the slide, place her at the top and down she goes. I am bored. Pity she can't just do the whole lot herself. Climb up, place herself at the top, she should surely be able to do that bit. I tell her what to do which she doesn't do because she can't understand me. I wish we were finished with the ming. Bad parent. Enjoy playing with your child. I wonder what happened next with Ozzie.

'Would you like to play in the sand with Ellie, Martha?' It works, they play away, I know I'll pay for it later in mucky boots. In I go and stand excitedly reading Ozzie. He gets the pig to go to the sheepdog and from the sheepdog to the duck and then he is down. He has convinced them all to do something for him, to bring him always to the next lowest animal and eventually gets down. I prefer wisdom to flying, it's better fun.

But the mom comes back, in the story that is, Ozzie's story. Very good she says to him, you got down. But the narrator tells us (as if Ozzie couldn't hear or didn't know or couldn't figure it out for himself) that she has been watching all the time and knows that he can't really fly. 'Now' she says, 'fly back up again.'

Frustrated and dejected I check on the girls. Muck and sand but no-one crying. I am cross with the mom. How dare she? Could she not just let him be clever, the flying will come in its own time. I am no longer concerned with the parallels with the morning, they broke down long ago, just cross with a parent who sets up her child.

'Dad. Will you wipe my bum?' 'Sure Ellen, but you were able to do that for yourself a year ago.' Frustrated and tired I give in to the day's chores and I cook, clean, pick up, put down, listen to the radio, my mind a numbness of essential trivia.

Later in the evening. Red wine and some space, I go back to Ozzie and read from the start, hoping to find something there, some key to the day's flux of feeling. I like Ozzie. I like anyone who wants to be wise, even if they can't fly. I read each page, slowly this time. I am shocked as I see the mom hidden on each page, I hadn't seen that earlier. She had watched him all the time, her controlling vigilance an affront to the chaos of my day. 'You set him up you bitch' I say out loud, 'You set out to catch him out. You just can't appreciate his creativity, his cleverness.' I am full of spite for a character in my child's book and am shocked at the feeling. Panopticon. The ever-present, not so benign parental gaze. I imagine Ozzie's shame and his fluster and I am contrite.

A sense of an ending, but an ending born of the need to end, the need for closure. The real ending is much more prosaic than that. Two weeks after the day in question I am outside with the girls again. Eighteen months old and Martha is climbing the climbing frame, rung by frightening rung and coming down the slide headfirst. Did I teach her or did she learn, I wonder? Was I right to set this up, will I now have to watch her, like Ozzie's Mom, every moment of her climbing life? I am terrified, but a secret part of me teacher, parent, father, supervisor, reader of texts, feels at ease again in the world.

I wrote *Lazy Ozzie* without any thought that it had any significance over and above a storied response to a tense situation. I saw it as a short story, as a piece of creative writing that I had written for myself. It was in my doctoral studies that the trouble started. As part of my participation on a doctoral programme I encountered the post-positivist, reflexive genre of Auto-ethnography and I began to see my story as being something of an auto-ethnographic account of my work as a research supervisor. I learned about auto-ethnography as 'a method and a text' (Etherington, 2004, p. 140), an autobiographical genre of writing and research that incorporates aspects of one's own life experience when writing about others (Etherington, 2004, p. 139). I could see *Lazy Ozzie* as 'a form of self-narrative that places the self within a social context' (Etherington, 2004, pp. 139-40).

I found it exciting to read Davies and Gannon make more ambitious, more radical claims for the genre of Auto-ethnography and of its value to my purpose of uncovering the subjective roots that reflexivity purports to expose. They claim that 'taking oneself and one's own ongoing experiences as the data' allows 'the richness, subtlety and complexity of the researcher's own embodied thinking and being in the world…[to] be told, brought to the surface of memory and language.' Auto-ethnography would allow me 'to make relevant those aspects of being that are suppressed by analytic strategies that draw a veil around emotions and bodies' (Davies and Gannon, 2006, p. 3).

I began to try to weave an argument about the emotional and relational dimensions of research supervision, using *Lazy Ozzie* as an auto-ethnographic illustration of a supervisor's own learning and development as a parallel to Janice's.

And so followed draft after draft of argument, poor Ozzie sitting unmoved and unchanged in the middle of each draft never getting even close to flying. Though hateful to revisit them, they are part of the story and this is an account of some of them.

Experts at Evidence-Based Research

The first draft tried to track my own experience of myself as a researcher and research supervisor in the context of changes and developments in the University sector. It cleverly, so I thought, presented a vignette from a Faculty meeting (8 May 2006) where faculty members had a strong reaction to new guidelines around research supervision coming from policy makers (Irish Universities Association, 2005). Some members at the meeting took issue with the insistence on the 'professionalisation of supervision' (NUIM, 2006) and drew the inference that current approaches to research supervision were being regarded as unprofessional.

I tried to plot some of the identity issues I encountered that I felt mirrored Janice's and went on to discuss them in the light of current thinking around Transformative Learning Theory (Mezirow, 2006; West 2006). Feedback was not positive. A colleague in the Department hated it and told me 'I almost completely disagree with your politics.' Feedback from my own supervisor mentioned that the academic discussion was somewhat pedantic. Nobody said anything nice about poor Ozzie.

I default on hard work and so it began. The next draft and the next, all accompanied by a persistent sense of dissatisfaction.

The Cambridge Introduction to Narrative

Then came summer holidays and I leave the office, feeling unusually well, mind you for the end of the academic year, and we spend, my family and I, a beautiful two weeks by the sea. In the relaxed empty spaces I revisit my literary studies of many years ago and read up on narrative and how it functions (Abbott, 2002). I get excited and take volumes of notes. I begin to understand how *Lazy Ozzie* works as a text and this is the answer to my questions. I write and write and feel I have now gone from 'monological' to 'dialogical' writing (Hunt, 2001). My happy days as an English teacher come alive and I imagine using my wonderful short story as a text with groups.

And so back in the office I write about how Lazy Ozzie works. The framing narrative (the supervisory meeting) and an embedded narrative (the reading of the story of Lazy Ozzie, a father playing with his children while he reflects on the story); narrative point of view, (homodiegetic narrator), themes and motifs, closure. I wrote about all of this and yet again felt that something, literally vital, was missing.

And then I met Davy Mc Bride and I felt that he could help.

The Other Side Of You: A Fictional Autoethnography

Davy is a character in Salley Vickers' novel *The Other Side of You* (2006) and the novel tells the story of his work with a patient Elizabeth Cruikshank who has attempted suicide. I liked him. I liked reading the ruminations about his own life and losses as he listened to hers. But I especially liked it that he makes an auto-ethnographic presentation at a medical conference and his presentation was all about the relational dimension of his work and the role of his own vulnerability in the healing process. I saw myself as Davy to Janice's Elizabeth. And his auto-ethnography said many of the things I wanted to say.

He decides to present a reflexive account of his work at the conference not out of enlightened thinking but as the result of a crisis. The night before the presentation he wakes up and realises he can't do it as planned:

> *It was a fastidious compilation of a couple of cases I'd treated over the past year, offering verbatim material of turning points in the treatment and a sound theoretical explanation of the underlying issues. It was well written, well argued and fundamentally false. I'd no appetite for reading the words I'd laboured over, still less for declaiming them in public, and given my present state it seemed likely that I would be in little position to do so.*
>
> (Vickers, 2006, p. 272)

He begins his lecture next day with a visual image, of Caravaggio's *The Supper at Emmaus* and uses it as a way in to the story of his work with Elizabeth Cruikshank which, he says, flowed 'unedited from my disencumbered heart' (2006, p. 274). He addresses his audience:

> *The history of my patient finally entrusted to me is not mine to divulge.*
> *It is another story. Hers. But I came to this conference with the intention of presenting a case history, or case histories, treated not by drugs but by other, less material, methods, and I mean not to fail in that undertaking. However, the case I wish to invite you to consider is not that of the suicidal patient I have been alluding to but my own, and the part played by Caravaggio's painting, and the story it portrays, in developing my understanding.*
>
> (Vickers, 2006, p. 275)

He writes about Caravaggio, too lengthy to reproduce here, but the conclusions he arrives at in his presentation spoke to me of what I hoped for my supervisee, that my mistakes and doubts and confusion might somehow not stand in her way, or better still, might actually be the source of something good:

> I believe that, in my dealings with this patient, nothing could have been accomplished without three factors: one, my own incompetence and attendant fear…two, my own desire to liberate myself from some long-term inner restriction…three my willingness to express my personal commitment to my patient's continued existence, which I did with uncharacteristic force.
>
> (Vickers, 2006, p. 275)

I concluded this particular draft by trying to see Davy (and I) as a practitioner/researcher who has had something of a qualitative researcher crisis. I quote from myself:

> In effect then he is concluding that his own countertransferential reaction, literally his story activated on listening to her story, was vital to the positive resolution to both stories. In a sense then, this fictional conference presentation performs, as it were, a researcher's crisis of representation (Holman-Jones, 2005), his decision to opt for providing an auto-ethnographic account of his research rather than blandly presenting the research itself, together with his argument that such a medium is the only method he could use in face of the relational dimension of the work.

And still I hadn't said what I wanted to say. Davy had not spoken for me, blast him, and I was still unable to speak for myself. I cut and paste. I rewrite. I shred copy after copy. I feel very young and confused and cannot understand what is happening me.

Confused or not the time came to send a second draft of my paper. The feedback I got, which I hated and agreed with in equal measure, says that the academic voice in the paper is 'frankly boring' and 'ponderous.' The day the feedback came happened to coincide with a meeting with John.

A Story of Two Pieces of Feedback

John's thesis had failed and he was hurt and angry. I wasn't his supervisor for the failed thesis, though I am now. How easy it was to have a similar conversation with him as I had with Janice. Structuring arguments, reviewing literature, building conceptual frameworks. I also talked to him about his passion, his strong feelings about rejection and failure, about what he really cares about in his thesis.

And then my own feedback arrived and I felt much of what he must have felt.

> *Blood and guts. That's what's missing. I am furious, enraged. Kicking
> and screaming as a result of my feedback. How dare he tell me it's boring,
> ponderous. I don't want to hear it. Don't want to feel this way.*

> *This is how Janice felt. This is how John felt this morning. Rage. The rage
> of being told by some supposedly benign and wise, superior being that I'm
> not good enough. They were raging with me. I'm raging with my feedback.*

> *So why do this to myself? Why write an auto-ethnography when I could easily
> find another university where the academic voice would be the one to hold
> sway? Why does Janice want to challenge herself? Why would John settle
> for an appealed pass when he could get so much more?*

> *Boredom with the old way of doing things. A feeling of there being something
> more, another way to think and write. I pontificate so often about the emotional
> dimension of teaching and learning and strive to include it. To honour the
> relational dimension of what we do. But here I am in it and I am full of rage.*

As I write in my journal the image of Ozzie's Mom comes to me. I see her as rigid, controlling and fundamentally stifling in her self-righteous position. I remember when writing the story, the experience of feeling similar to her and hating that in myself, hating that feeling. And so I realise that she is something of an objective correlative for me, an external manifestation of this drab and lifeless academic voice that I have built and walled myself in with. Vigilant, correct, compliant, well meaning, but hardly benign for all of that.

Tired and Terrified

> *When you are tired or terrified
> your voice slips back into its old first place
> and makes the sound your shades make there...*

(Heaney, 1984, p. 52)

Regression is the process of returning to an earlier place in oneself, usually as a result of a crisis or a transition (Mander, 2000, p. 17). As Heaney has it we return there when tired or terrified and we encounter old ghostly voices. Object Relations theory (Gomez, 1997) tells us that the voices we encounter are those we have internalised during the process of development, or those we have developed to help us to cope early in life. So Ozzie, for example, may always hear a stern, controlling voice when he is learning something new. He may even develop that voice himself to help him feel in control of a fragile ego. If reflexivity is demanded of him, then these things will out.

The process of reflexivity that this paper has involved has been somewhat convoluted and tortuous. I have been tired and terrified. I have crashed the brand new family car. I have lost my way (literally and metaphorically) on well-known roads. I have been preoccupied, trying to work out what I want to say, how to say it. And I have retreated betimes to the stronghold of a dispassionate, controlled academic voice.

This voice has many antecedents in my own personal story, some of them inchoate, some more accessible. The theme of the story has been one of a conflict between compliance and creativity, between safety and risk. The ghostly personae have included a 13 year old rebellious teenager; a 16 year old who discovered poetry; a young undergraduate who, suspecting he was not as clever as the others, floundered in the morass of a final year dissertation; a 22 year old accident victim who felt punished by the universe for not being 'good enough', who threw himself earnestly into academic work. Each of these positions, I am sure, harbour younger personae too, Martha's or Ozzie's age, all equally struggling to survive and thrive.

Crossing the Lines of Self-defence

Your story took so long
The plot was so intense
You took so long to cross
The lines of self-defense

(Cohen, 2006, p. 209)

Speedy talks about the way post-modernity has eroded authoritative traditions, giving us space to 'speak with less authority about smaller parcels of knowledge-in-context and to tell more local stories' (2005, p. 63). This paper started life as a story together with various commentaries written in a standard academic register: an attempt to eschew traditional research methods while holding on to an authoritative voice. As the paper grew, however, out of the fertile liminal space (Speedy, 2007) between writer and reader it has mutated. What has emerged from this is a local story of how my author/ity has been eroded, making way for new possibilities as a (less authoritative) research supervisor and as an author.

Making the Familiar Strange

Conclusions are a funny business in writing. The conclusion is the place where very often we are tempted to adopt the 'godlike' academic voice that is 'stripped of all human subjectivity and fallibility' (Richardson, 1997, p. 18) and we propound our final thesis. Alternatively conclusions are the formulaic place where we 'say what we have just said.' Whichever course I take I am at this point supposed to say that reflexivity is indeed a demanding process and that we should recognise this and legislate for it in how we write and think about a radical approach to adult education.

But this paper is just a story and endings are just conventions. In her discussion about reflexivity in research, Ryan talks about the way that poetry, visual arts, novels and so on can 'make the familiar strange' (2006, p. 26). Reflexivity is, above all, a way of making something familiar strange, a way of being in something and outside it at the same time. This story has been a way to be in the struggle with reflexivity and to witness it reflexively at the same time.

Stories, however, need readers:

> [stories] long to be used rather than analysed; to be told and retold rather than theorized and settled; to offer lessons for further conversation rather than undebatable conclusions; and to substitute the companionship of intimate detail for the loneliness of abstracted facts.

(Ellis and Bochner, 2000, p. 744)

And so, having read this now another story begins.

References

Abbott, P.H. (2002). *The Cambridge introduction to narrative.* Cambridge: Cambridge University Press.

Chase, S. (2005). Narrative inquiry, multiple lenses, approaches, voices. In N. Denzin, & Y. Lincoln (Eds.), *The Sage handbook of qualitative research*, (3rd ed.). London: Sage.

Cohen, L. (2004). *The book of longing.* London: Viking Penguin.

Coleman, M. & Williamson, G. (2004). *Lazy Ozzie.* London: Little Tiger Press.

Davies, B. & Gannon, S. (2006). The practices of collective biography. In B. Davies & S. Gannon, *Doing collective biography* (pp. 1-15). Maidenhead: Open University Press.

Davies, B., Browne, J., Gannon, S., Honan, E., Laws, C., Muller-Rockstroh, B. & Bendix Peterson, E. (2006). The ambivalent practices of reflexivity. In B. Davies & Gannon, S. (Eds.), *Doing collective biography* (pp. 88-113). Maidenhead: Open University Press.

Ellis, C. & Bochner, A. (2000). Autoethnography, personal narrative, reflexivity: Researcher as Subject. In N. Denzin & Y. Lincoln (Eds.), *The Sage handbook of qualitative research* (2nd ed., pp. 733-768). London: Sage.

Etherington, K. (2004). *Becoming a reflexive researcher.* London: Jessica Kingsley.

Gomez, L. (1997). *An introduction to object relations.* London: Free Association Books.

Heaney, S. (1984). *Station Island*, London: Faber and Faber.

Holman Jones, S. (2005). Authoethnography: Making the personal political. In N. Denzin & Y. Lincoln, (eds.). *The Sage handbook of qualitative research* (3rd ed., pp. 763-792). London: Sage.

Hunt, C. (2001). Assessing personal writing. In *Auto/Biography*, 9(1 & 2), pp. 89-94.

Irish Universities Association. (2005). *Reform of 3rd level and creation of 4th level Ireland: A framework proposal submitted by the Irish Universities Association.* Dublin: IUA.

Kenny, E. (2006). Learning to care: Adult education and gendered occupations. Unpublished MA Dissertation, NUI Maynooth.

McGlynn, W. (2006). The role of the university in challenging inequality in higher education. Unpublished MA Dissertation, NUI Maynooth.

Mezirow, J. (2006). An overview on transformative learning. In P. Sutherland & J. Crowther (Eds.), *Lifelong learning: Concepts and contexts* (pp. 24-38). London: Routledge.

Mander, G. (2000). *A psychodynamic approach to brief therapy.* London: Sage.

National University of Ireland (2006). Minutes of the Faculty of Arts, 8th May, 2006.

Richardson, L. (1997). *Fields of play: Constructing an academic life.* Piscataway, NJ: Rutgers University Press.

Richardson, L. & St. Pierre, E. (2005). Writing: A method of inquiry. In N. Denzin & Y. Lincoln (Eds.), *The Sage handbook of qualitative research* (3rd ed., pp. 959-978). London: Sage.

Ryan, A.B. (2006). Post-Positivist approaches to research. In M. Antonesa, H. Fallon, A. B. Ryan, A.

Ryan & T. Walsh (Eds.). *Researching and writing your thesis: A guide for postgraduate students* (pp. 12-26). Maynooth: MACE.

Speedy, J. (2005). Writing as inquiry: Some ideas, practices, opportunities and constraints. *Counselling & Psychotherapy Research*, *5*(1), pp. 63-4.

Speedy, J. (2007). Reflexivities, liminalities and other relationships with the space between us. In J. Speedy, *Narrative inquiry psychotherapy*. Houndsmills: Palgrave Macmillan.

St. Pierre, E. (1997). Circling the text: Nomadic writing practices. *Qualitative Inquiry* 3(4), 403-417.

Vickers, S. (2006). *The other side of you.* London: Fourth Estate.

West, L. (2006). Managing change and transition: A psychosocial perspective on lifelong learning. In P. Sutherland & J. Crowther (Eds.), *Lifelong learning: Concepts and contexts* (pp. 39-47). London: Routledge.

Zagajewski, A. (2004). *Selected poems*, London: Faber and Faber.

Beyond the Third Way: New Challenges for Critical Adult and Community Education

BRID CONNOLLY
NUI MAYNOOTH

Beyond the Third Way: New Challenges for Critical Adult and Community Education

BRID CONNOLLY
NUI MAYNOOTH

Introduction

In the mid-nineties, when I was trying to make convincing connections between community development and adult education, the neo-liberal tendencies in the sector profoundly disturbed me. All over Ireland, local and community development groups were springing up, developing strategic plans for their areas. While some of these plans were genuinely consultative and indisputably concerned with poverty and inequality, many were purely economic, demonstrating little concern for social issues. The elements of the neo-liberal tendencies included the alliance with *The Third Way*, the neo-liberal ideology of economics, which entails going beyond Left and Right, and promoting the 'what works' strategy. Giddens has been highly influential in devising this ideological strategy, laying the foundation for the emergence of New Labour type politics that has prevailed in Ireland, the UK and the USA under Clinton (Giddens, 1994). However, this centrist positioning overtly supported corporate power, at the expense of the poor, and pushed the privatisation of all kinds of services, such as the health service, to the detriment of the public service. A key example in Ireland was the privatisation of the telecommunications services. The short-term effect was to substitute communal ownership with corporate ownership and shareholders, but in the long term, outcomes to the service users are disastrous. No broadband nationally, high prices for terrestrial communications and the highest costs in Europe for mobile phone users.

However, with the benefit of hindsight, it is possible to see that these economic plans did indeed help to revitalise an Ireland that was overwhelmingly damaged by unemployment and emigration. In these days of full employment, it is difficult to believe that, in the mid-eighties, a quarter of a million people were officially unemployed; two hundred thousand people had emigrated; and many women were not eligible to sign on the live register of unemployment. But it is important to remember that, simultaneously, women's community education had entered a new era. Funding mechanisms from Europe, such as New Opportunities for Women (NOW), or philanthropic foundations such as Allen Lane, which seamlessly connected with the existing community education programmes, supported this sector fundamentally. National organisations, such as AONTAS were quick to recognise this trend and highlighted it in various ways. The Department of Adult and

Community Education in Maynooth had already played a substantial role in the development, offering a programme of critical courses and politicised tutors (Ryan & Connolly, 2000). Tellingly, these politicised tutors carried critical discourses into community education, especially through the processes and methods of critical pedagogy, and influenced it profoundly. This article will explore this phenomenon, looking at the sources of politicisation, and connect it with the communitarianism of development in Ireland over the past ten years or so.

Communitarianism is often seen as the social arm of neo-liberal economics. However, communitarianism has very different emphases, focusing as it does, on the communal over the individual, and the issues of poverty and inequality over consumerism and market forces. This focus on a just and fair society is contingent on the philosophical and ethical commitment to civil, social and cultural rights for the population. This is all the more stark when we consider that the strong emergence of neo-liberal economics over the past ten years in Ireland is often accompanied by regret for the breakdown of community. We have smirked to ourselves when Fianna Fáil invited Robert Putnam over to speak at its think tank on building communities. But the government has failed to recognise the interconnectedness of ideology: it is not possible to promote, privilege and show absolute partiality towards the individualism of neo-liberalism economic capital on the one hand, and to simultaneously promote the collectivity and mutual interdependence of social capital on the other.

In many ways, the partnerships of the past ten years have fallen into this trap. Partnerships were established as a way of formalising the existing community development processes, and linking them with other social actors, such as employers, politicians, social services providers, and so on. The aim was to capture the energy of the movement, and direct this energy into regeneration and community building. They are aiming towards a sustainable community enterprise model of development. However, in many ways, partnerships were established without building the safeguards of the just society. Further, the government has entrusted the partnerships with the task of solving enormous social problems. For example, widespread drug misuse is out of control now, with devastating consequences for families, communities and neighbourhoods and leading to organised crime on a scale never before witnessed in Ireland. But this is a societal problem, and community development is not equipped or resourced to tackle it in the long term. Social capital is the key to maintaining democracy and building participation in civil society (Putman, 2002), but active citizenship in Ireland is now reduced to Tidy Towns committees and participation in Neighbourhood Watch. These, of course, are important for social cohesion, but they do not succeed in addressing the real problems in society, such as poverty, educational disadvantage, environmental degradation and social exclusion. Rather, this model of participation and active citizenship has the effect of diverting attention away from these problems and absorbing huge community energies.

This article will look at neo-liberalism, and examine how it co-opts popular movements, such as community development. I will explore critical adult and community education and the part it could play in building a communitarian model of community development, enabling people to develop a critical analysis of neo-liberal development. In particular, it will look at critical pedagogy as the most essential component of praxis, the key route to transformation and consciousness raising.

Critical Pedagogy

For me, adult and community education centres on the work of Paulo Freire, especially *The Pedagogy of the Oppressed* (1972). His ideas have been very influential along two strands, that is, via Henry Giroux's critical pedagogy in mainstream schooling (2006), and bell hooks' feminist pedagogy (1994). Giroux must be read in the company of Peter McLaren (1989). These US voices have few counterparts in Ireland. In Ireland, mainstream pedagogy is based on what Freire calls 'the banking system'. That is, it is based on a relationship which involves:

> a narrating Subject (the teacher) and patient, listening objects (the students). ... The teacher talks about reality as if it were motionless, static, compartmentalized and predictable. His (sic) task is to 'fill' the students with the contents of his narration...(Freire, 1972, p. 45)

Notwithstanding his use of the male pronoun, Freire's analysis of the teacher/student relationship encapsulates the model that is most familiar, whether it refers to the sociology lecturer in the theatre at university or the mathematics teacher at the chalk board in secondary school. This relationship is essentially hierarchical, authoritarian, and undemocratic, but this ideology of pedagogy is suppressed in the familiar and unquestioned disconnection between theory and practice. Definitions of pedagogy locates it as a science of methods, which avoids an ideological analysis, common in science orientated epistemology. This means that pedagogy is regarded as neutral, non-controversial and unproblematic. Adult and community education argues against this, proposing an alternative social analysis of pedagogy and education.

This alternative social analysis on the role of education is illuminated in Kathleen Lynch's *The Hidden Curriculum* (1989) where she argues the key role that education plays in the reproduction of the status quo, in the Irish context. Lynch asserts that a sociological analysis of the Irish education system shows that it did not contribute to a significant redistribution of resources (1989). She continues this work in *Equality in Education* (1999) where she affirms that part of the problem in tackling the issue of inequality is the inability of sociology to look at equality outside of the liberal framework, and selective mobility, inherent in equal opportunities, has reinforced structural inequalities. She promotes the notion of critical theory as a way forwards, and she maintains that 'critical educational theory is a very real attempt to present a model of explanation which incorporates a theory of praxis-orientated action' (1999, p. 79).

However, she argues that critical education theory has not liaised with normative moral and political theory. This means that there is no vision for an alternative future, no proposal as to how a just and equal society might look. However, a feminist perspective may suggest what is possible, as we look at the profound changes emanating from the women's movement on both personal and social planes; and a feminist critical education analysis may be the key to offering alternative concrete policy and political implications. While the focus of my interest is on critical pedagogy in adult and community education, I want to review the overarching lifelong learning context.

Lifelong Learning

Lifelong learning has acquired a new profile in the European community. The development of policy in lifelong learning demonstrates a new role for lifelong learning in the knowledge society and the information economy. The spotlight on lifelong learning has illuminated the part that adult and community education has played in developing human and social capital, and how flexibility and openness have contributed to making learning attractive (Commission of the European Communities, 2005, p. 5). In addition, the European community is contextualised within other agencies concerned with democracy, social inclusion and economic development, particularly the Organisation for Economic Co-operation and Development (OECD). The OECD has been highly influential in sponsoring lifelong learning as a key conduit to the knowledge society and the information economy. It holds that lifelong learning is a key element in fostering democratic participation and citizenship, as well as social and economic well-being (OECD, 1996). The definitions of lifelong learning are varied, but the OECD definition is useful:

> [Lifelong learning includes] all purposeful learning, from the cradle to the grave, that aims to improve knowledge, and competencies, for all individuals who wish to participate in learning activities. (OECD, 2004, p. 1)

The distinguishing features of the vision for lifelong learning include: a systemic, cross sector, view; a view that accords centrality to the learner and motivation to learn; and finally, recognition of the multiplicity of educational goals, including personal development, knowledge development, economic, social and cultural objectives. These goals overlap with my vision of adult and community education, though not completely. I feel that it is useful to connect my area of interest, to the wider thinking in lifelong learning, as Skilbeck emphasises the importance of the way in which lifelong learning is carried out. He says that it should be 'inclusive, attractive, accessible, well-articulated, of high quality and relevance – and appropriate in…functioning, content and style to all learners (2001, p. 56).

That is, if the lifelong learning agenda is expanded into third level education, it would necessarily entail a shift from traditional pedagogy, to this more fluid, inclusive and learner-centred model. This is still a long way from critical pedagogy, but it is very interesting to see the shift away from traditional models towards the adult and community education model. This necessarily entails the repositioning of academics, so as 'to achieve a more open style of operation and closer integration with the community' (2001, p. 14). Simultaneously, the European Commission focused on basic skills, targeting the most educationally disadvantaged among the populations.

The European Commission set in motion the subsequent development of lifelong learning with *Memorandum on Lifelong Learning* (2000) making the case for the promotion of lifelong learning with emphasis on six areas, again echoing the interests of adult and community education:

■ Basic skills, focusing not just on adult basic education, but also on multi-lingual, ICT, and other key competences;

■ Investment in human development, especially in relation to human resources;

■ Innovation in teaching and learning, with particular focus on adult education methodologies;

■ Valuing learning for its own sake;

■ Rethinking guidance and bringing it into the realm of what adults might need for balanced living, rather than the existing concentration on adolescents' vocational needs;

■ And finally, bringing learning out of the institutions and into the community, closer to home and the workplace. (Commission of European Communities, 2000, p. 2)

These priorities elicited a number of responses, which praised the memorandum on its breadth of vision, but cautioned against the overwhelming pull of the market. For example, the report from Ireland, following a round of consultations, re-iterated the role of philosophy and guiding principles that ought to underpin the practice of lifelong learning as promoted in the memorandum. It also emphasised the need to give weight to active citizenship, as the ultimate desirable outcome of lifelong learning, and employment skills as secondary outcomes. In addition, it recognised that there was a lack of attention to the issue of equality. The Irish submission (COM, 2001) shows the ideological position of lifelong learning in Ireland, putting it firmly on the side of the poor and disadvantaged, and the Commission in the *Communication*, shows that this point was taken seriously:

There were, however, concerns that the employment and labour market dimensions of lifelong learning were too dominant within the definition. Indeed, in relation to specifying the objectives of lifelong learning, responses tended to echo the Memorandum as well as citing wider aspects such as the spiritual and cultural dimensions of learning. Overall, consensus can be surmised around the following four broad and mutually supporting objectives: personal fulfilment, active citizenship, social inclusion and employability/adaptability. (Commission of European Communities, 2001, pp. 16-19)

These political and philosophical dimensions are essential if lifelong learning is to be reflexive, as it becomes more institutionalised: dimensions that it looks for in learners. Thus, the promotion of lifelong learning could, if supported, bring reflexivity about, as a norm. This would mean that the wherewithal to constantly review itself is built in. This quality is essential, as lifelong learning is embedded in policy development in Europe, with the Lisbon Strategy and the Bologna Process. The Lisbon Strategy, formulated in 2000, holds that economic growth, social inclusion and sustainable development are contingent on the knowledge society, and has devised an agenda for lifelong learning to promote learning. This strategy has underpinned the developments in individual EU countries, and has been very influential in setting the agendas on national development plans. Further, it has connected civil society with the economy inextricably, a result that is positive in bringing the economy out into the public domain, where it can be scrutinised and regulated more closely. That is, the economy has been perceived as being governed by irrefutable internal laws, such as the law of supply and demand. In civil society these laws can be interrogated, especially in relation to initiatives such as fair trade, or minimum wages. Thus, the Lisbon Strategy, by promoting learning as participation in civil society, has, intentionally and unintentionally, incorporated a built-in process of evaluation and review.

The Bologna Process, again underpinned by the lifelong learning agenda within the knowledge society, focuses on the Universities, and their role in constructing the knowledge society. A key outcome of the Bologna Process is the Qualifications Framework, which aims to provide an internationally recognised framework of educational credentials. The effects of this framework is to have transparency across the continent, a key solution to the elitism of the traditional qualifications pathways, highly dependent on traditional learners, and very resistant to the needs of non-traditional learners.

This means that lifelong learning takes a foothold in the formal system. Alongside this, it has provided a recognisable umbrella for adult and community education, together with an implicit acknowledgement of the value and worth of the processes and methods that makes adult and community education so effective. In addition, adult and community education has long promoted access and support for non-traditional learners in third level education, but it has taken the lifelong learning agenda to guarantee this. Thus, while the policy development in lifelong learning has been driven by the emergence of the knowledge economy, the policy proliferation has created a fertile ground on which adult and community education can grow and flourish. But the policy proliferation must be welcomed with caution, to ensure that adult and community education is not press-ganged into another agenda. The next section will take a closer look at the Irish context, to examine it in the light of the principles and philosophies which provide the milieu for adult and community education. These European policy developments frame this context, yet there is a clear distinction between the Irish and the European cases.

The Irish Context

Following on from European policy development, this section will explore policy papers as a prelude to more academic literature. It is heartening to see that the White Paper on Education (Department of Education, 1995) maintains the commitment to redistribution through education. It re-asserts this function, with particular emphasis on minority and disadvantaged groups, and how education ought to be concerned with justice and equality for them. However, the culture of inequality is more pervasive than the political will to implement the policies set down in the White Paper, and there is very little evidence that the goal of equality is on the real agenda:

> In contemporary Ireland, the signs, sounds and symbols of conspicuous consumption, market forces and materialistic secularism abound; they have been described recently as 'turbo-capitalism'. (Sugrue, 2004, p. 1)

This is the context for these educational reviews that have taken place over the past ten years or so. While some attention has been paid to social justice, particularly as a socialist Minister for Education, Niamh Breathnach, was responsible for shaping the White Paper, in 1995, the system has proved remarkably resistant to social transformation. Sugrue continues: 'despite the depth of dialogue…more deeply embedded educational structures have remained remarkably resistant to change (2004, p. 6).

Instead, Lynch maintains that those concerned with inequality are removed from government policy implementation, and further, that they are not able to propose alternatives to mainstream education that would bring about more equal outcomes (1999, p. 24). In addition, her powerful work, from ten years previously, which highlighted the issues addressed in the White Paper, shows that the embedded inequalities perpetuate themselves in the hidden curriculum, the main conduit being the ways in which education is conducted (1989).

The main conduit for policy implementation in Ireland, over the past ten years, has been a social process called partnership. The partnership process developed within the community sector, particularly with the emergence of the communitarianism. Communitarianism has attempted to chart a course between Left and Right wing politics. The concept of communitatianism has been developed over the past 20 years or so (Bell, 1993). The model of responsibility to and for one another is central to the concept, and it proposes a code of ethics based on this responsibility, rather than, for example, religious morality. It encompasses the rights based codes of liberal humanism, but goes beyond them, in attempting to build active citizenship, social obligation, and self-reliance. In Ireland, we have seen community responses to many of the issues in society, that have emerged as the outcome of the state's inability to address or to cope with difficulties inherent in modern society (Ó Cinnéide & Walsh, 1990). It is an alternative to the harshness of individualism, and it fosters self-expression and self-determination.

Community development, as the grassroots activity that has applied communitarian ideology, has been a very powerful agent in raising issues around social and cultural inequality, such as poverty, discrimination, neglect, and other disadvantages. Community development essentially entails members of a community – geographical or issue-based – identifying their needs in terms of development, sustainability and education, and collectively working together to meet those needs. The processes integral to community development provided a blueprint for partnership. The Irish Government co-opted these processes in the national development plans for social and economic progress. These national plans filtered into all corners of Irish public life. The Irish Government views it as a consultative and negotiation process which takes over from the traditional adversarial processes. Social partnership is concerned with economic and social progress, and it centres on four pillars: the Trade Unions, Employer and Business, Farming, and Community and Voluntary, with which the Government negotiates. These pillars seem to be socially inclusive, and a lot of attention is paid to 'soft skills' such as team building and trust. It includes group development, familiar to all of us in adult and community education, with an emphasis on inclusion and influence in decision making. However, a brief review indicates that the Government has plans to expand and develop the partnership approach:

> *The use of the full range of available [through partnership, of] joint problem solving, decision-making and group development processes varies significantly between committees, with some being very advanced and innovative and others considerably less so. Generally, these new processes are quite under-developed and under-used.*

> (*http://www.bettergov.ie/index.asp?docID=184* accessed 25th November 06)

The success of the Irish economy has obscured the ideology which underpins the partnership approach. The preoccupation with the economy has over-ridden all other considerations, and the partnership approach puts the stamp of approval on it. This is in spite of the silenced voices, particularly women's groups, minority groups, and people from disadvantaged backgrounds. In addition, in Ireland, we are closer to the USA economic model, than the European one of welfare and social care, and this emerges through the normative discourses, unbidden, in the consultation process within partnership. Further, there is a strong anti-intellectual strain in partnership, which Sugrue and Gleeson attribute to the pragmatism adopted by Irish society since the foundation of the state in 1922 (2004, pp. 277-279). Further, they continue with the connections between ideology and the lack of progress in promoting equality and justice in the education system. They identify elements of the hidden curriculum in a number of dimensions.

> It is necessary therefore, particularly in relation to curriculum reform to delve even deeper into the substance and process of reform to identify continuities as well as changes wrought through partnership to explore the very notion of partnership and the extent to which it has promoted more inclusive participation and more democratic decision-making.

(2004, pp. 6-7)

Another dimension Sugrue and Gleeson examine is that of the conflation of the knowledge society and the knowledge economy. They provide a useful thumbnail distinction, courtesy of Hargreaves (2003): 'The knowledge economy serves the private good. The knowledge society also encompasses the public good' (p. xvi). However, any attempt to address the public good through the curriculum have been robustly resisted, (Sugrue & Gleeson, 2004, pp. 284-286), in favour of the standardised measurement system culminating in the Leaving Certificate. This resistance is located within a number of contexts through the absence of debate, or, as Sugrue and Gleeson name it, silences and virtual silences. They include teacher training and teachers unions, parents associations, the discourse of anti-intellectualism and the dominance of the centre right ideology in policy implementation (2004, pp. 293-301). Traditionally, teacher education was controlled by the Roman Catholic Church, with the main intention to perpetuate Irish catholicism, against the trend of secularisation. In addition, the feminisation of the profession has led to the reduction of status. The feminisation has not been accompanied by feminist changes; rather it has led to regression to traditional gender roles, and the perception that schooling is an extension of the domestic domain, rather than a public community activity, the most significant connection for children and adolescents with civil society. Lynch and Lodge also worry about the increasing alienation from learning by the students coming from second level. This applies even those who 'do well', i.e. those who get the high marks, and manage to register for the University courses of their choice. This alienation is evident almost immediately on leaving school, coming from a system which promotes conformity, standardisation, and control over creativity, innovation and critical thinking (2002).

Finally, Sugrue and Gleeson identify the lack of research around education as crucial in maintaining silence. This point demonstrates the status of education in the overall social agenda. There is very little funding for research, and whatever resources are available are put into investigating what works, rather than any critique or questionings of assumptions or approaches, focusing on good news. They found that there is little or no commitment to informing debate and policy decision-making. In addition, they maintain that classrooms and schools continue to be 'secret gardens', with the consequence that no reform is possible when teaching stays within the four walls (2004, pp. 301-303). The desire to open up the practice of teaching through research has led to the narrow classroom focus: how to improve practice and how to improve the teacher/student relationship. While this is an improvement, taking the practice out of the private domain and into the public, it has the effect of taking the focus off the role of education in society. This necessarily entails a form of double bind. It colludes with the discourse of standardisation and measurement, and supports the co-option of education for the knowledge economy.

The struggle to reclaim education for the public good is taking place between a small number of critical educators against the large number of common sense politicians and powerful partners in the mainstream arenas. Adult and community education, on the other hand, is a marginal arena, and it has an array of fora for discussion of the very topics that are silenced in the mainstream. This is due, in part, to the politicisation of the key players: the participants. An emancipatory ideology, rather than the more reforming ideology of *The White Paper on Education* (DE, 1995), underpinned the *White Paper on Adult Education*, (DES, 2000). This was both following the current trends in the field, as well as shaping the future. For example, the consultation rounds before the White Paper on adult and community education, included a large number of groups and networks committed to the social justice model of adult and community education. AONTAS, The National Association for Adult Education; NALA, The National Association for Adult Literacy; The Shanty Educational Project, committed to social transformation; several women's community education networks as well as a huge number of participants contributed to this consultation round (DES, 2000). There are no such organisations within mainstream education, and participants – students – are particularly silenced, deferring to parents' associations, which are more committed to the *status quo*. In addition, the teachers' unions are more committed to employment conditions, which has of course served the sector well, but it is more resistant to critiquing the profession *per se*, and they are frequently at odds with an emancipatory processes prevalent in adult and community education. Adult and community education is explicit in its commitment to educationally and socially marginalised groups, and this shapes the field. Freire's theory and practice is concerned with these groups. In contrast to mainstream education, critical adult education approaches are vitally important, and the voices of critical educators are heard in all the learning sites: in the national organisations; in the training of adult educators; among the participants; and among the organisers and facilitators.

This critical voice is recognised in the larger sociological community, in addition to the educational community. For example, Tovey and Share acknowledge the growth in adult and community education as rapid and significant (2003, pp. 197-199). Lynch perceives it as pivotal in community development, (1997, p. 118) and it is seen as a positive alternative to the inflexible, conservative mainstream schooling system (Hannan *et al*, 1998, p. 127). Indeed, adult and community education has more in common with new social movements than with societal institutions. Groups such as workers groups, unemployment groups, community development groups, the Irish Traveller Movement, the women's movement, and gay rights movement are underpinned by liberation ideology. Adult and community education has been significant within these groups, as well. This sector is part of the communitarian trend. Identified in the US, by Etzioni (1993, cited in Powell and Geoghegan, 2004, p. 1), it has a different history in Ireland, beyond the scope of this article. However, from the late 1980s, many Freire-inspired groups in disadvantaged communities promoted it. It was supported by the state, particularly by the Combat Agency, and was advocated as the middle ground between right and left. The key to communitarianism is that power is distributed into communities, be they geographical or interest led. The members of the community identify their needs and work collectively to meet those needs (Kelleher and Whelan, 1992). Adult and community education is central to this process, and in this environment, the critical dimensions of the field are embedded in the practice. The next section will look at the sources for politicised community activities, and locate the field of adult and community education within this milieu. In this, critical theory and new social movements provides the most fertile ground for the development of the seeds for the community strand of the sector, while the women's movement is the source for the radical learning dimensions.

Sources for the Politicised Dimensions of Adult and Community Education

New Social Movements

Freire's thinking (1972) has embedded critical pedagogy in adult and community education, while mainstream education has resisted any attempts to transform the pedagogical approaches which interfere with the private transactions within the classroom. Critical pedagogy in adult and community education has the explicit and particular intention of enabling disadvantaged people to claim their civil status in an envisioned just and equal society. In contrast with the old social movements' theory, taking the labour movement as an example, new social movements are more likely to be gender, age or race/ethnicity based, and are more likely to have to have their political sites in civil society, rather than state and mainstream politics. They are more likely to be ethically based, rather than interest based, and are by and large non-hierarchical, relying on networking and informal organisation, instead. Further, they are less concerned with sectional interests and more interested in values, ideals and an envisioned fairer and just society (Tovey & Share, 2003, pp. 449-451). Tovey and Share contextualise Habermas' contribution, in their analysis of the late modern Ireland, in terms of the youth, peace and ecology movements (Habermas, 1987, cited in Tovey and Share, 2003, p. 452), which are congruent with adult and community education. The concept of 'lifeworld' is very useful here. Lifeworld includes the everyday interpersonal relationships, within and outside of the family, where we are orientated towards mutual understanding and common ground. This concept is very useful in helping to explain the trends in new ways of living, in relationships and in developing the self. The emergence of new social movements can be seen as a response by the lifeworld to the threat of colonisation by the forces of the economy, by the objectification of the population, and other forms of domination and coercion, (Tovey & Share, 2003, p. 452). However, a number of new social movements have an alternative ideology, with an avowedly explicit agenda of rolling back the advances emanating from the liberatory social movements. For example in Ireland, a great proportion of the Pro-Life movement are people under the age of twenty-five, and the most public face of it is Youth Defence:

> Youth Defence modelled itself on the tactics of Operation Rescue type groups in the U.S. On marches they chanted "we don't need no birth control, hey Taoiseach leave the kids alone". They leafleted on Saturdays in the city centres with gruesome pictures of supposed abortions. They picketed TD's houses, including those of Nuala Fennell and Eamonn Gilmore. They rang in death threats to Radio Dublin when it wouldn't carry interviews with them. Pro-choice campaigners, in one incident, were attacked with pick-axe handles and snooker cues resulting in broken bones. Youth Defence marches were 'stewarded' by hired heavies (complete with wrapped knuckles).

(http://flag.blackened.net/revolt/ws93/abortion38.html accessed 25th November 06)

These reactionary social movements have an ethical underpinning, but do not have a liberatory ethos, and they grow in the same milieu as adult and community education. However, their conservative ethos counters the possibilities for social transformation. The development of the reactionary ethos is of deep concern for those of us passionate about critical education, and the part that it could, if nourished, play in supporting change.

The reliance on neo-conservative right-wing thinking for the modus operandi of organisations like Youth Defence demonstrates the type of jungle in which the human freedom movements find themselves. I find it is most illuminating to look at the Critical Pedagogy website, to see the connections between social movements, civil society, and education:

> The primary characteristic of this school of thought (critical theory) is that social theory, whether reflected in educational research, art, philosophy, literature or business, should play a significant role in changing the world, not just recording information.

> (*http://www.perfectfit.org/CT/ct1/html*, accessed 25th November 06)

The links between critical theory and the practice of new liberatory social movements are difficult to trace. There is little doubt that new social movements have the capacity to mobilise populations of people with raised consciousness, ethical positions and reflexivity. Ultimately, despite operating outside of the traditional political pathways, new social movements achieve political objectives, and indeed, as Tovey and Share maintain, they have managed to redefine politics itself (2003, p. 456). An example from the ecology movement which has persuaded the state to become involved in recycling and reducing waste. In Ireland plastic bags are levied, against the pressure from industry, but to great popular success.

> Writers from the European tradition now recognise that social structural or ideological characteristics of societies are not sufficient to explain the emergence and development of specific NSMs [new social movements].

> (Tovey & Share, 2003, p. 456)

When we look at adult and community education through the lens of new social movements, I think it helps to position it more clearly in society. That is, the actuality of adult and community education is outside of the traditional models of social institutions. The emphasis on dialogue and common understandings; underpinned by ethical considerations such as respect for difference and diversity; driven by the key players; and devoted to growth and development, and fulfilling the potential of all the participants, are the major characteristics of adult and community education. We can see it both as an example of new social movements in its own right, and also as the key route to enabling people to gain the understandings of the same social movements. In this dual role, it has gathered a momentum as a force for social change, and in doing so, it is fulfilling its stated and implicit objectives, that of social transformation. It has also a key role in personal change. In order to look at this more closely, I will now consider the influence of critical pedagogical thinkers before moving on to feminist scholars, and the women's movement, by reviewing the position of critical research and epistemology in the adult and community education arena.

Critical Pedagogy

While education for democracy has been part of the agenda for many years, increasingly, mainstream education has become commodified, as a product to be consumed, rather than a process to be undertaken. As such, the status it holds in Irish society is that of training for professional occupation, the main route to privilege and resources for most people. In the area of adult and community education, though, there is strong resistance to the push for credentialisation, at the expense of emancipation. Freire (1972) has been the key influence in the field of adult and community education, in Ireland. Since the foundation of this field in the community, through the literacy movement, and in higher education, with the establishment of post-graduate education for educators programmes, Freire's liberation theology and Marxism has been the guiding vision (see for example, Connolly, 2003). Freire's concepts of conscientization and praxis have underpinned the pedagogy in adult and community education, gradually gaining recognition for the effectiveness in liberatory education. However, the position of critical pedagogy in mainstream Irish education is very marginal, and critical educators have not had the same impact as journalists and commentators such as Fintan O'Toole. However, educators such as Henri Giroux have arguably developed a profile among critical thinkers in the US.

> The critical question here is whose future, story and interests does the school represent… Critical pedagogy argues that school practices need to be informed by a public philosophy that addresses how to construct ideological and institutional conditions in which the lived experience of empowerment for the vast majority of students becomes the defining feature of schooling.
>
> (http://www.perfectfit.org/CT/giroux1.html accessed 25th November 06)

He asserts that critical pedagogy attempts to create new knowledge though the emphasis on interdisciplinary thinking, taking into account the lived experience of people. It is fundamentally an ethical positioning, which locates itself around the categories of race, gender, class and ethnicity in these experiences (2005). This follows from Freire's conscientization, spelling out with more clarity – and including the issue of gender which Freire completely ignored – the elements involved in reflection on ones' own experiences. This also parallels the most basic process in the women's movement, that of consciousness raising, and the generating of new ways of knowing. Giroux recognises that Freire was crucial in shaping theoretical stances in areas such as post-colonial studies, critical adult and community education, and the primacy of politics in education. Further, Freire was not simply proposing a method; rather he placed the onus on the educator to generate knowledge. However, his lack of awareness of gender was a major flaw (hooks, 1994). He exhorted educators to be broader intellectuals, not technicians. Most crucially, he revitalised the relationship between theory, practice and the struggle for social justice (Giroux, 2005). This point is crucial, in terms of the role of the educator.

Increasingly, the educator is the purveyor of methods devised to carry out a curriculum, which is formulated in terms of what society needs. This generally refers to the economy, and I will look at it in the Irish context. However, the point here is that educators are devalued in their intellectual role, and re-valued as report writers and assessors of learning. Apple views this technical role as part of the overall decline of education as liberation, and the promotion of education as 'something one purchases – the school itself is turned into a lucrative market' (1986, p. 163). Further, the market/consumer dynamic pushes the individualistic trend to the logical end-point, that of the disconnection with the social and cultural context. It is most difficult to generate class/race/gender consciousness with the meritocratic system, and yet, the meritocratic system is perceived as the fairest way in which to distribute educational advantage. McLaren perceives that it is the role of the critical pedagogue to forge this link, to work as an educator to bring in the social and cultural into the individual learning experience (1989, p. 230). Thus, the role of critical pedagogy is to develop the educator as theorising intellectuals, and to develop in the students, a critical consciousness in the process of education. This links it with critical epistemology, underpinned by critical research. In the next section, the part of feminist scholarship is examined.

Feminist Scholarship

The concept of the lifeworld is very useful in focusing on the main dimensions of adult and community education. Concerned as it is with the minutiae of everyday, (extra)ordinary living, the face-to-face realities of interpersonal relationships, it provides the wherewithal to study this sphere of human life. When 'turbo-capitalism' operates in this world, it objectifies people and reduces them to consumers, helpless in the maelstrom of market forces. Yet it is this very site that adult and community education is most concerned. The feminist slogan, 'the personal is political' could be the mantra for this sphere. Adult and community education reclaims the personal from the consumer/client/customer domains, for the domain of active citizenship and agency. 'All personal change is a form of learning or questioning' (Williamson, 1998, p. 172).

Adult and community education is much more than the continuous development of skills; it embraces self-knowledge, covering both thoughts and feelings about who we are, free from social prescriptions like class and race. The forms of self-understanding open to us are both private and public, part of the wider cultural discourses on identity and experiences. The differences in roles and identities reflect much more than the functional importance attached to them, and the exercise of power by the power elite is ultimately decisive in attributing status and value to those roles (Williamson, 1998, pp. 173-174).

When women's community education started in the early 1980s, the ways of working, the content of the programmes and the learning environments were radically different to anything that had gone on in Ireland before. It seemed to be a very feminine set up, with loose, informal networks allowing the entire phenomenon to develop. The lived experience of the participants was the fundamental starting point. Most women did not identify with the women's liberation movement, which they perceived as removed from their lives. This (mis)interpretation was fed by media ridicule of the movement, while, in reality, women were beginning to enjoy the benefits of the changes, such as contraception, work outside the home, and the notion of childcare (Connolly, 2003). However, the net impact of the women-led project is the proliferation of the feminist dimensions, which subverted the traditional, hierarchical, and conventional models of adult education. That is, feminist methodologies emerged, underpinned by distinct feminist epistemologies. Stanley and Wise were pioneering feminist sociology in Higher Education, from the 1980s onward, yet it was more evident in the marginal world of adult and community education. Stanley and Wise advocated feminist research in order to create the common ground for academic acceptance and social power, and contributed hugely to the development of feminist ways of knowing (1993). Their insights and arguments are particularly pertinent in looking at critical adult and community education, with the stance that feminist theory should be at some level consonant with experience, that the researcher (educator) is on the same critical plane as the participants, and that 'reality' is constructed by the subject (p. 200). This is congruent with Luke and Gore, who say:

> As feminist educators, we all attempt...to create pedagogical situations which 'empower' students, demystify canonical knowledges, and clarify how relations of domination subordinate subjects marked by gender, ethnicity, class, sexuality, and many other markers of difference.

> (1992, p. 1)

Feminist research inherently captures the dramatic decline in the absolutes of positivism and rationalism. Lather welcomes the notion of research as praxis, the direct linking between theory, practice, and reflexivity (1991, p. 50-51). This again is congruent with the possibilities in adult and community education, and has the potential to disrupt the old orders. Luke and Gore add a perspective on male critical educators, which brings us back to Giroux and McLaren.

> But in the process of trying to create emancipatory classrooms, we have come up against 'uneasy' readings:...our readings of where feminist educational work stands in relations to male-authored critical pedagogy.

> (Luke and Gore, 1992, p. 1)

Their uneasiness lies in finding themselves as feminist educators within patriarchal systems of knowledge, scholarship and pedagogical relations. This resonates with Stanley and Wise, and with my own experience as a feminist educator. In spite of the rhetoric and the profile of educators such as Giroux, critical pedagogy has not made an impact in education in any real way (Kanpol, 1999, pp. 1& 185). Critical pedagogy is still embedded in patriarchal relations, silencing the feminist voices, or at least marginalising them. In addition, critical pedagogy is enmeshed in systems that have been staunchly resistant to human freedom and liberatory change, such as global capitalism; or they have incubated grass roots movements, using the learning from civil rights movements, etc. dedicated to rolling back the advances made over the past forty years or so. Feminist critical educators could demonstrate a new way of working, working alongside allies in the field of adult and community education.

Conclusion

The key focus of this article is on the growth of neo-liberal ideology in social life and the ways in which neo-liberalism has co-opted the trends in adult and community education in order to further its own economic agenda, subduing counter-cultural critical voices in the process. Further, it proposed that communitarianism has been supported in national strategic plans in order to mitigate the worst effects of neo-liberalism without constraining or regulating the market economy. Finally, it suggests that it is still possible to reclaim the progress of the knowledge society for the benefit of civil society rather than the economy, through the work of critical pedagogy and drawing on liberatory social movements and feminist scholarship.

In the article, I sketched the wide scope of the adult and community education world, drawing on the influential policy formation role in the European Community and Commission, particularly, and the texts derived from the newly emerging interest in lifelong learning. The review then focused on the Irish context, which has been highly influenced by the developments in Europe, but with a clear distinct identity, probably unique to Ireland, due to history and culture. The context in Ireland is illuminating, in that mainstream education is in a severe crisis at present, and critical educators are almost completely voiceless in the debate. However, adult and community education is an arena which subverts the traditional boundaries, crossing between communitarianism, new social movements, and feminist critical education. Critical adult and community educators are optimistic and confident that social transformation is not only possible, but the struggle for liberation strengthens the resolve to bring about a just and equal society.

References

Bell, D. (1993). *Communitarianism and its critics.* Oxford: Clarenden Press.

Commisson of the European Communities. (2005). Communication from the Commission, *Mobilising the brainpower of Europe: enabling universities to make their full contribution to the Lisbon Strategy.* Brussels: COM.

Commisson of the European Communities. (2001). *Report on the Irish Consultation Process.* Brussels: COM.

Commisson of the European Communities. (2000). *A Memorandum on Lifelong Learning.* Brussels: COM.

Connolly, B. (2002). *Adult education for politicisation.* Unpublished research for MEd.

Connolly, B. (2003). Women's community education: Listening to the voices. *The Adult Learner, Journal of Adult Education in Ireland.*

Department of Education. (1995). *Charting our education future: White paper on education.* Dublin: The Stationery Office.

Department of Education and Science. (2000). *Learning for life: White paper on adult education.* Dublin: The Stationery Office.

Etzione, A. (1993). *The spirit of community.* New York: Touchstone.

Freire, P. (1972). *Pedagogy of the oppressed.* Harmondsworth: Penguin.

Giddens, A. (1994). *Beyond left and right: The future of radical politics.* Standford. CA: Stanford University Press.

Giroux, H. (1992). *Border crossings.* London: Routledge & Kegan Paul.

Giroux, H. (2005). *What is critical pedagogy? URL: http://www.perfectfit.org/CT/giroux1. html* accessed 25th November 06.

Gramsci, A. (1971). *Selection from prison notebooks.* London: Lawrence and Wishart.

Hargreaves, A. (2003). *Teaching in the knowledge society.* Buckingham: Open University Press.

Hannon, D., McCabe, B. & McCoy, S. (1998). *Trading qualifications for jobs: Overeducation and the Irish labour market.* Dublin: ESRI/Oak Tree Press.

Hooks, b. (1994). *Education as freedom.* New York: Routledge.

Hughes, C. (2002). *Key concepts in feminist theory and research.* London: Sage.

Kanpol, B. (1999). *Critical pedagogy: An introduction* (2nd ed.), London: Bergin & Garvey.

Keddie, N. (1980). Adult education: An ideology of individuation. In J. Thompson (Ed.), *Adult education for a change*. London: Hutchinson.

Kelleher, P. & Whelan, M. (1992). *Dublin communities in action.* Dublin: Community Action Network/Combat Poverty Agency.

Kristeva, J. (1986). *The Kristeva Reader.* Oxford: Blackwell.

Lather, P. (1991). *Getting smart: Feminist research and pedagogy with/in the postmodern.* London: Routledge.

Luke, C. & Gore, J. (Eds.). (1992). *Feminisms and critical pedagogy.* London: Routledge.

Lynch, C. (1997). Literacy is a human right: An adult underclass returns to education. In E. Crowley & J. MacLaughlin (Eds.), *Under the belly of the tiger: Class, race, identity and culture in the global Ireland.* Dublin: The Irish Reporter.

Lynch, K. (1989). *The hidden curriculum: Reproduction in education – A reappraisal.* London: Falmer Press.

Lynch, K. (1999). *Equality in education.* Dublin: Gill and Macmillan.

Lynch, K. & Lodge, A. (2002). *Equality and power in schools.* London: Routledge/Falmer.

McLaren, P. (1989). *Life in schools.* New York: Longman.

Middleton, S. (1993). *Educating feminists: Life histories and pedagogy.* New York: Teachers College Press.

Ó Cinnede, S. & Walsh, J. (1990). Multiplication and division: Trends in community development since the 1960s. *Community Development Journal*, 25(4).

Organisation for Economic Co-operation and Development. (2004). *Policy brief: Lifelong learning.* Paris: OECD.

Organisation for Economic Co-operation and Development. (1996). *Making lifelong learning a reality for all.* Paris: OECD.

Powell, F. & Geoghegan, M. (2004). *The politics of community development: Reclaiming civil society or reinventing governance?* Dublin: Falmer.

Putnam, R. (Ed.). (2002). *Democracies in flux: The evolution of social capital in contemporary Society.* Oxford: Oxford University Press.

Ryan, A. B. (2001). *Feminist ways of knowing: Towards theorising the person for radical adult Education.* Leicester: NIACE.

Ryan, A. B. & Connolly, B. (2000). Women's community education in Ireland: The need for new directions towards 'really useful knowledge.' In J. Thompson (Ed.). *Stretching the academy: The politics and practice of widening participation in higher education.* Leicester: NIACE.

Skilbeck, M. (2001). *The university challenged: A review of international trends and issues with particular reference to Ireland.* Dublin: HEA.

Sugrue, C. & Gleeson, J. (2004). Signposts and silences: Situating the local within the global. In C. Sugrue (Ed.), *Curriculum and ideology: Irish experiences, international perspectives.* Dublin: Liffey Press.

Sugrue, C. (Ed.). (2004). *Curriculum and ideology: Irish experiences, international perspectives.* Dublin: Liffey Press.

Thompson, J. (1996). 'Really Useful Knowledge': Linking theory to practice. In B. Connolly, T. Fleming, D. McCormack & A. Ryan (Eds.), *Radical learning for liberation.* Maynooth: MACE.

Tovey, H. & Share, P. (2003). *A sociology of Ireland* (2nd ed.). Dublin: Gill and Macmillan.

Weiner, G. (1994). *Feminisms in education: An introduction.* Buckingham: Open University Press.

Williamson, B. (1998). *Lifeworlds and learning: Essays in the theory, philosophy and practice of lifelong learning.* Leicester: NIACE.

URL: http://www.bettergov.ie/index.asp?docID=184 accessed 25th November 06

URL: http://flag.blackened.net/revolt/ws93/abortion38.html accessed 25th November 06

What if Education Mattered?

ANNE RYAN
NUI MAYNOOTH

What if Education Mattered?

ANNE RYAN
NUI MAYNOOTH

Introduction

Inclusiveness and widening participation, terms that were once confined to the lexicons of adult educators, are now commonly used by the providers of formal education. Their interest stems from a realisation that retaining relevance in a rapidly changing economic, social and educational environment calls for:

- broadening the student constituency base;

- rejuvenating the range and content of courses on offer;

- enabling student movement between courses and between providers and

- redefining the broader developmental agenda of education in terms of not only personal development but also communal well-being.

There is no dispute that education plays a significant role in determining an individual's life chances and choices. There is also ample evidence that broad-based access to education contributes to social cohesiveness and stability.

This article assumes that education matters, that its primary purpose is individual and social emancipation, that it must attend in equal measure to the social, cultural and economic well being of all, and that success is measured by the extent to which all sectors of the population are equipped with the analytical and strategic skills necessary to articulate their needs and negotiate their futures. This article assumes that:

> *There is no such thing as a neutral education process. Education either functions as an instrument that is used to facilitate the integration of the [learner] into the logic of the present system and bring about conformity to it or it becomes the practice of freedom.*

> (Freire, 1972, p. 56)

The article calls for an analysis of conventional approaches to today's usage of the term widening participation, especially in third level education, with a view to recapturing the overtly political agendas original embedded in the term. It argues that without this analysis, interventions to widen participation may serve to bolster, rather than reform, an educational system that has to date spectacularly failed to serve the needs of so many.

Reading an Unmapped World: Literacy Class, South Inner City

One remembers welts festering on her palm
She'd spelt 'sacrament' wrong. Seven years of age,
preparing for Holy Communion. Another is calm
describing the exact humiliation, forty years on, the rage

at wearing her knickers on her head one interminable day
for the crime of wetting herself. Another swears she was punch drunk
most of her schooldays – clattered about the ears, made to say
I am stupid; my head's a sieve. I don't know how to think

I don't deserve to live.
Late November, the dark
chill of the room, Christmas looming and none of us well fixed.
We bend each evening in scarves and coats to the work
of mending what is broken in us. Without tricks,

without wiles, with no time to waste now, we plant
words on these blank fields. It is an unmapped world
and we are pioneering agronomists launched onto this strange planet,
the sad flag of the home place newly furled.

(Meehan, 2000, p. 51)

In this poem Paula Meehan captures not only the powerlessness these women experienced during their schooldays but also their determination to make meaning of their harsh experiences – a determination that adult educators encounter so often in learners who were poorly served by the formal education system. In that chilly room the poet and the women are engaged in an emancipatory process. Meehan includes herself in the endeavour. She is not a detached professional delivering a service. She is a co-learner, an active participant in unveiling their world and intervening to reclaim their right to be subjects of that world rather than objects of an educator's actions (Freire, 1994, p. xi-xii).

Learning to read one's world involves comprehending the social and cultural forces that cause oppression and inequality. Freire (1994, p. xii) makes the point that educators who want to educate in this way must resist pragmatism;

For educational pragmatists, there are no more dreams. Likewise there is no more reading the world. The new educational pragmatism embraces a technical training without political analysis, because such analyses upsets the smoothness of educational technicism. ...To the educational pragmatist, other social and critical preoccupations represent not just a waste of time but a real obstacle in their process of skills banking.

For those, like Meehan, who resist pragmatism 'Pedagogy is a matter of principle and purpose rather than mere technique' (Crowther et al., 2000, p. 174).

The purposefulness of this pedagogy is to empower the educator and the learner to affect the kind of change that involves intervention in the system rather than compliance with it. The educator and the learner have to look inward to reveal the constellation of beliefs and values that shape their personal interpretations of the world. The pursuit of such a pedagogy includes, but goes beyond, creating an environment where learners can transcend the emotional and intellectual stagnation that often results from negative educational experiences. 'Principle and purpose' demand a level of engagement that stretches outward further than the immediacy of a group of learners, to include an engagement with the wider contexts that cause exclusion.

This article explores the nature of the challenges posed by such a pedagogy.

Approaches to the Problem of Exclusion

Although today's schoolrooms are no longer beset by the overt violence described in Meehan's poem, current statistics highlight on-going failures on the part of the formal education system to meet the needs of particular learners, for example 22 per cent of young people leave school early; 55 per cent of adults aged between 16 and 64 have literacy difficulties (Morgan, et al., 1997); one in ten children leaving primary schools have literacy problems (Kellaghan, 2002); people with disabilities make up over 8 per cent of the population but account for only 1.1 per cent of the student population in third level (AHEAD, 2004).

How we respond to statistics such as these is determined by the conceptual frameworks we draw on to give meaning to the phenomenon of exclusion. According to Tett (2006, p. 22), a particular conception of what the problem is, and consequently how it is to be solved, becomes dominant and that makes it difficult to see that there are alternatives. Being critically conscious of our conceptual frameworks and those of the system in which we operate, makes it possible to search for alternatives.

Liberal and Radical Approaches to Exclusion

Approaches to exclusion	Liberal	Radical
Perspective on problem	Unfortunate occurrence	Predictable occurrence
Location of the problem	Excluded individual/group	Education system
Motivation to intervene	Compassion/opportunity to increase numbers of entrants	Human Rights/justice
Desired outcome	Increase numbers of those entering and staying in the system	Address structural inequalities in mainstream services
Main concern	Maintain integrity of the education system	Respond to learner's needs
Role of the educator	Transmit knowledge	Create knowledge
Strengths	Public appeal. Measurable	Distinguishes causes from symptoms
Weaknesses	Focus on how exclusion manifests itself	Threatens existing system. Hard to measure success

(Based on Ryan, 2000, p. 42)

This chart considers two possible conceptualisations of exclusion. The first column presents a liberal perspective that is largely in keeping with current trends in targeted funding to redress the problem of exclusion at third level. The second column draws on a radical adult education analysis. Oppositionalities are not always useful in enabling the kind of dialogue necessary to reveal the nuanced issues that invariably inhabit complex problems such as exclusion, however, in this instance they serve to expose how an unquestioning acceptance of the status quo can focus attention on the symptoms of exclusion rather than the causes and in so doing compensate for, rather than challenge, the deficiencies of the system.

Perspectives on the Problem of Exclusion

An approach to exclusion that sees it as an unfortunate or haphazard occurrence '...treats education as an autonomous site with an ability to promote equality internally irrespective of external forces' (Lynch, 1999, p. 309). It obscures the deep rooted, systemic and self-perpetuating nature of exclusion and the embeddedness of education in that cycle. A national survey on new entrants to higher education highlighted the importance of socio-economic status in determining the success or failure of individuals within the education system. This survey noted '...persistent social inequalities...reflected in the over-representation of the children of certain groups among new entrants to higher education, relative to their shares of the population' (O'Connell et al, 2006, p. 136). The implied under-representation of other sectors of the population echoes an earlier study that found the following:

■ Students from lower socio-economic groups were significantly less likely to complete second level education;

■ Those students from lower socio-economic groups that sit the Leaving Certificate tended to achieve significantly lower grades, and

■ For students with modest levels of performance in the Leaving Certificate, those from higher socio-economic groups had a higher transfer rate to third level.

(Report of the Action Group on Access to Third Level Education, 2001, p. 34)

These statistics suggest an educational system that pushes out, or keeps out, significant numbers of people, the majority of whom are the most vulnerable to start with. The findings also imply an education system that compounds rather than compensates for existing disadvantages.

A study of graduates in Scotland found that when it came to employment, graduates from disadvantaged families received lower net financial returns than their more advantaged counterparts (Furlong and Cartmel, 2005). This study infers that despite interventions designed to enable disadvantaged individuals acquire degree level qualifications, socio-economic backgrounds continue to play a significant role in determining the subsequent employment chances of graduates.

An approach to exclusion that acknowledges the economic and power inequalities at play outside the education system is better positioned to understand the nature and scale of the problem and to consider the values, beliefs, assumptions and practices that shape and sustain an education system that does not or cannot serve the interests of particular groupings.

Location of the Problem

When the problem of exclusion is located in those who are under-represented, then these individuals and groupings become the main focus of attention. The reasons why they are excluded are attributed to their failure to engage appropriately with the system (Tett, 2006). This failure is put down to factors such as a lack of motivation to participate on their part, little encouragement from peer group and family, and financial constraints. This analysis is particularly evident in third level access programmes. Students who enter institutions via these initiatives are categorised as 'mature' students, students with 'special needs' or disabilities, and 'non-traditional' students. Once these students have gained access, special supports are put in place to retain them within the system. Such supports again focus on these students' differences in terms of how they process information, or respond to established teaching and examining procedures, and life style issues such as their need for childcare or wheelchair ramps. These differences are not seen as a resource to be drawn upon but as deficiencies to be rectified. Access to education under these conditions implies a degree of benevolence on the part of a system that accommodates these 'outsiders' as exceptional cases.

If, on the other hand, the problem is located in the system, then the focus of attention shifts away from '…integrating *deficient* people…' (Crowther et al, 2000, p. 179) and towards identifying the deficiencies of the system. This approach is concerned with knowing how the system works, how it reflects and reproduces existing inequalities in society and revealing the values that sustain it. It raises questions as to who benefits from how the system currently functions and what motivates the financial investment and effort on the part of educational institutions that seek to 'fit' individual students into the existing system.

Motivation for Intervention

Education up to a certain level is widely accepted worldwide as a human right. UNESCO produces an annual *Education for All Global Monitoring Report* that tracks the progress of individual countries towards this goal. Agencies such as UNESCO invariably justify their call for universal education on social and economic grounds. The benefits to the individual, while recognised, are less compelling than the correlations between education and good health, longer life expectancy, environmental protection, etc. In addition the term lifelong learning, for all its many shortcomings and disputed meanings, challenges the notion that learning is confined to a particular stage in life. Nevertheless, despite the dominance of these conceptual frameworks, the amount of education one has a right to remains problematic and ill-defined. This is particularly evident when it comes to third level education. It could be argued that in the poorer countries of the world the right to education at third level is less than pressing when such very large numbers of children and adults have no access to even the most basic primary level education. However, the question of how much education one has a right to, is also problematic in the rich countries of the world such as Ireland, where there is no such excuse. Over the past five years EU agreements and numerous reports on the practices in third level education have urged the sector to undertake deep-rooted changes to the structure, content, methodology, purpose, delivery and nature of the system with a view to providing for a wider constituency (Corradi et al., 2006).

Notwithstanding these calls for reform, efforts to tackle inequality in third level education in Ireland remain grounded in a conceptualisation of education as a privilege rather than a right. Investment in widening participation has resulted in providing opportunities that can only be availed of by '...a small minority of relatively advantaged people within a given disadvantaged group' (Lynch, 1999, p. 309). Those who are deemed to be most able within such groups are given access while the remainder continue to be excluded. Recent trends among universities to set strategic goals that aim to attract 'high quality students' are particularly worrying. Implicit in this aim is a sense that there are 'low quality students' out there that these same institutions have little interest in accommodating. In such a climate the rhetoric of widening participation appears to be about increasing the pool of potential students from among those who can be moulded to 'fit' the needs of the institution. It offers little or no indication that these institutions are keen to tackle the more complex underlying causes of exclusion.

The Primary Concern

Those whose primary concern is to 'fit' otherwise excluded students into the system tend to be concerned with maintaining the integrity of the system, in particular to maintaining existing standards. One aspect of the 'maintaining standards' discourse is a concern not to 'over-advantage' non-traditional students through the provision of supports. A concern of this nature is only meaningful in the context of the competitive dimension of student performance in examinations. This assumes that ranking students according to their relative performances is a worthy educational aim and that a 'level playing field' is a realisable or desirable condition for the provision of education.

The radical response to exclusion has no commitment to maintaining the integrity of the system. On the contrary, if the problem is endemic in the system, then unless the system is fundamentally reformed, it will continue to exclude in ways that are eminently predictable. If the values that underpinned past practices and that resulted in excluding certain groups of learners are the same as the values that underpin current practices that seek to include some members of these groups, this constitutes an unchanged elitist stance.

The Role of the Educator

The role of the educator is significantly different within the liberal or radical conceptual framework. A liberal perspective accepts the current parameters that define worthwhile knowledge. Although research conducted within this perspective may dispute the validity of aspects of this knowledge and/or seek to build on the existing knowledge base, the broad parameters of what is deemed worthy of attention are determined by a limited number of publishers, journals and academic institutions. Those who do not have access to these channels or whose ways of knowing do not conform to traditional academic practises, have little opportunity to influence the knowledge creation process.

The radical approach is concerned to establish academic practices that are inclusive and open-ended, capable of democratising the process of knowledge creation and in so doing seek to establish forums where all of the stakeholders, particularly those who are not well served at present, can play an active part in refashioning the provision of educational services. Forums of this nature are needed at the levels of policy-making and co-ordination of provision as well as at the level of implementation.

Until diversity is nurtured as a source of strength, initiatives designed to widen participation are in danger of perpetuating an approach to education where all but a selected few of those who are different remain excluded and those who are deemed worthy of inclusion are corralled and manipulated until they conform to the mainstream ideal.

References

Corradi, C., Evans, N. & Valk. A. (Eds.). (2006). *Recognising experiential learning: Practices in European universities.* Estonia: Tartu University Press.

Crowther, J., Martin, I. & Shaw, M. (2000). Turning the discourse. In J. Thompson (Ed.), *Stretching the Academy: The politics and practice of widening participation in higher education* (pp. 171-185). Leicester: NIACE.

Freire, P. (1972). *Pedagogy of the oppressed.* Harmondsworth: Penguin.

Freire, P. (1994). Foreword. In D. Macedo, Literacies of power (pp. xi-xii). Oxford: Westview Press.

Furlong, A. & Cartmel, F. (2005). *Graduates from disadvantaged families: Early labour market experiences.* Bristol: Joseph Rowntree Foundation/The Policy Press.

Kellaghan, T. (2002). Approaches to problems of educational disadvantage. In *Primary education ending disadvantage. Proceedings of the National Forum* (pp. 17-30). Dublin: St Patrick's College.

Lynch, K. (1999). *Equality in Education.* Dublin: Gill and Macmillan.

Meehan, P. (2000). *Dharmakaya.* Manchester: Carcanet Press.

Morgan, M., Hickey, B. & Kellaghan, T. (1997). *International Adult Literacy Survey: Results for Ireland.* Dublin: The Stationery Office.

O'Connell, P. J., Clancy, D. & McCoy, S. (2006). *Who went to college in 2004?: A national survey of new entrants to higher education.* Dublin: Higher Education Authority.

Report of the Action Group on Access to Third Level Education. (2001). Dublin: Stationery Office.

Ryan, A. (2000). Peripherality, solidarity and mutual learning. In J. Thompson, (Ed.), *Stretching the academy: The politics and practice of widening participation in higher education* (pp. 36-53). Leicester: NIACE.

Tett, L. (2006). *Community education, lifelong learning and social inclusion.* Edinburgh: Dunedin Academic Press.

In Mindful Search of a Good Theory of Learning at Work

ANNE MURPHY
DUBLIN INSTITUTE OF TECHNOLOGY

In Mindful Search of a Good Theory of Learning at Work

ANNE MURPHY
DUBLIN INSTITUTE OF TECHNOLOGY

This chapter considers the need for higher education to seek a revised set of theories which reflects how learning actually happens in the world of work. It makes a case for an approach to understand learning at work and to understanding contemporary knowledge production within a more expansive analytical framework than is evident in current techno-rational discourses of higher education policy with regard to informal and non-formal learning. It suggests that emerging paradigms of learning will oblige traditional higher education and adult learning practices to question most of their assumptions about worker-learners and will alter the future nature of their relationships with them within the new locus of knowledge production: the workplace.

Introduction

The scholarly literature of work-based learning broadly divides adult educators locally and globally into two main camps: the access and widening participation camp, frequently driven by a liberal humanism agenda of social justice and inclusion and which does not necessarily challenge the power and status of the academy, and the more critical radical camp which seeks the democratisation and legitimation of all knowledge with parity of respect for different ways of knowing (Carlson and Apple, 1998; Kincheloe, Steinberg and McLaren, 1999). Fenwick (2002) argues that seeking to understand work-based learning and working knowledge presents significant challenges for traditional modes of learning and for the role of the adult educator. Her review of the literature revealed that work-based learning theorists variously emphasise the socio-cultural aspects of learner-worker identity and context (du Gay, 1996; Edwards, 1998; Kincheloe, 1999), or philosophical aspects (Billett, 1998, 2001; Beckett and Hager, 2001; Hager, 2002) or aspects of complexity of contexts and relationships (Schön, 1987; Rogoff, 1990; Valera, Thompson and Rosch, 1990; Lave and Wenger, 1991; Davis and Sumara, 1997). Additionally, the literature reveals that practical pedagogical aspects of work-related learning are being variously theorised by Illeris (2004), Boud (2005) and Eraut (2002, 2005).

Radical educators, however, generally distance themselves from the discourses of learning at work framed by practices of mainstream human resource development and from discourses reflecting neo-liberal agendas in higher education. Instead they seek spaces for resistance and for counter-hegemonic influence (Ryan, 2001; Lynch, 2006).

Within those spaces are sites where theories of non-academic learning are emerging: theories which need to be both contextually sustainable and philosophically acceptable to practitioners and policy makers alike. Those theories seek re-discovery of a post-industrial and postmodern public sphere where learning outside the academy is legitimated in its own right and not solely in relation to the hegemonic constructs of an elite system which is being forced by expediency to engage with such learning. So, legitimate questions at this juncture might be as follows: is there sufficient common space among divergent theories to name a good theory of learning at work which could inform further and higher education policies and practices? or, as practitioners, are we working from unquestioned assumptions based on tacit, unproblematic understanding?

Assumed Shared Meanings About Learning at Work

The predominant EU and national policy discourses seeking to inform contemporary further and higher education practices with regard to the nature and status of learning in the workplace generally define such learning in terms of its differences from traditional education and training. The nomenclatures of *non-formal* and *informal* learning are now firmly established in policy rhetoric with little variation in definition or effort to seek depth of understanding. *Formal* learning is generally assumed to be structured and intentional learning which has a programme, teaching, assessment and certification. A further assumption is that informal and non-formal learning is residual, is what is left when formal learning is factored out. This way of understanding the terms seems unproblematic and technically efficient at first, and it is the understanding that underpins most institutional approaches to distinguishing among the different forms of learning for the purpose of academic recognition and certification in higher education. It is also the definition underpinning EU supports for recognition of experiential learning as it is articulated in the 2001 Communication on Lifelong Learning as follows:

> **Formal learning:** *learning typically provided by an education or training institution, structured (in terms of learning objectives, learning time or learning support) and leading to certification. Formal learning is intentional from the learner's perspective.*

> **Non-formal learning:** *learning that is not provided by an education or training institution and typically does not lead to certification. It is, however, structured (in terms of learning objectives, learning time or learning support). Non-formal learning is intentional from the learner's perspective.*

Informal learning: *learning from daily life activities related to work, family or leisure. It is not structured (in terms of learning objectives, learning time or learning support) and typically does not lead to certification. Informal learning may be intentional but in most cases it is non-intentional (or 'incidental'/random)*

(2001. pp. 32-33)

Cedefop (2003) offered the following definitions of the terms as cited in the glossary attached to EU Document, 3 March, 2004 *Common principles for validation of non-formal and informal learning*:

Formal learning: *Learning that occurs in an organised and structured context (in a school/training centre or on the job) and is explicitly designated as learning (in terms of objectives, time or learning support). Formal learning is intentional from the learner's point of view. It typically leads to certification.*

Non-formal learning: *Learning that is embedded in planned activities and not explicitly designated as learning (in terms of learning objectives, learning time or learning support), but which contains an important learning element. Non-formal learning is intentional from the learner's point of view. It typically does not lead to certification.*

Informal learning: *Learning resulting from daily work-related, family or leisure activities. It is not organised or structured (in terms of objectives, time or learning support). Informal learning is in most cases unintentional from the learner's perspective. It typically does not lead to certification.*

The National Qualifications Authority of Ireland (NQAI) (2005) definition of non-formal and informal learning in its policy document, *Principles and Operation Guidelines for Recognition of Prior Learning in Further and Higher Education June 2005*, below, is close to the EU 2000 definition:

formal learning *which takes place through programmes of study or training that are delivered by education or training providers, and which attract awards.*

non-formal learning *that takes place alongside the mainstream systems of education and training. It may be assessed but does not normally lead to formal certification. Examples of non-formal learning are: learning and training activities undertaken in the workplace, voluntary sector or trade union and in community-based learning.*

informal learning *that takes place through life and work experience. (And is sometimes referred to as experiential learning.) Often, it is learning that is unintentional and the learner may not recognise at the time of the experience that it contributed to his or her knowledge, skills and competences.*

The EU, CEDEFOP and NQAI definitions above presume shared acceptance of all that is implicated in the terms used. While there indeed may be a shared general acceptance of the EU definition, it is also reasonable to test if the literature from education practice generally complies with the definition.

In 2002 the UK Learning and Skills Development Agency (LSDA) commissioned a report which would offer conceptual clarification on definitions and issues related to non-formal and informal learning. An interim consultation document was published electronically by the researchers, Colley, Hodkinson and Malcolm in 2003 and a final report in 2004. They consulted literature across the English speaking world and used it to present some of the nuances not suggested in the EU definition of terms. The LSDA review of the literature found that, in a large number of cases, definition of terms was assumed. In other cases there was little agreement around how the terms should be defended, bounded and used. Sometimes there was overlap: other times disagreement. The writers identified twenty overlapping factors which distinguished formal and non-formal learning as different, and twenty-three factors for possible ideal types of formal and non-formal learning. Their interim list of factors is reproduced below.

Criteria and Characteristics of Non-Formal Learning

The LSDA researchers collapsed the criteria into four main dimensions: process, location and setting, purpose, and content, as a means of capturing the essence of differences in practice between formal and non-formal learning, accepting that neither category of learning is a discrete entity, that elements of the non-formal informal permeate all formal learning processes, and that a focus on inter-relationships would serve understanding better than a focus on divergence. The report additionally found that types of learning carried value assumptions, either implicitly or explicitly, with one form or the other being viewed as inherently, and sometimes morally, superior.

A further complicating factor for the researchers in arriving at definitions was where elements of formal, structured learning were included in what were categorised as informal structures, such as in-service training at work, in social learning context such as community-based education where there were direct inputs, and in youth development work where there were elements of formal mentoring. The use of formal and informal learning within radical adult education traditions was found to be intertwined with professional practice in the field, while in mentoring of disaffected youth the formality of the learning was coloured by the political intent of the intervention. A key dimension in both these examples was defined as the significance of unequal power relations and the pervading influence of politics both at the micro and macro levels.

Interim List of Factors Distinguishing Formal and Non-Formal Learning

	Distinguishing criteria of non-formal learning	Ideal type of formal learning	Ideal type of non-formal learning
1	Teacher-learner relations	Teacher as authority	No teacher involved
2	Location (education or community premises)	Educational premises	Non-educational premises
3	Learner/teacher intentionality/activity (voluntarism)	Teacher control	Learner control
4	Extent of planning or intentional structuring	Planned and structured	Organic and evolving
5	Nature and extent of assessment and accreditation	Summative assessment/ accreditation	No assessment
6	External determination or not	External determined outcomes/objectives	Internally determined objectives
7	Purposes and interests to meet demands of dominant or marginalised groups	Interests of powerful and dominant groups	Interests of oppressed groups
8	The nature of knowledge	Open to all groups, according to published criteria	Preserves equality and sponsorship
9	Whether learning is seen as embodied or just 'head stuff'	Propositional knowledge	Practical and process knowledge
10	The status of the knowledge and learning	High status	Low status
11	Education or non-education	Education	Not education
12	Part of a course or not		
13	Whether outcomes were measured	Measured outcomes	Outcomes imprecise/ un-measurable

	Distinguishing criteria of non-formal learning	Ideal type of formal learning	Ideal type of non-formal learning
14	Whether learning is collective/collaborative or individual	Learning predominantly individual	Learning predominantly communal
15	The purpose of learning	Learning to preserve status quo	Learning for resistance and empowerment
16	Pedagogical approaches	Pedagogy of transmission and control	Learner-centred, negotiated pedagogy
17	The mediation of learning – by whom and how	Learning mediated through agents of authority	Learning mediated through learner democracy
18	The time-frames of learning	Fixed and limited time-frame	Open-ended engagement
19	The extent to which learning is tacit or explicit	Learning is the main explicit purpose	Learning is either of secondary significance or is implicit
20	The extent to which learning is context-specific or generalisable/transferable	Learning is applicable in a range of contexts	Learning is context-specific

The LSDA report examined formal and non-formal learning as complex paradigms and uncovered degrees of superiority of one over the other over time. For instance, they argued that late twentieth century values favour high status, rational and scientific, generalisable and portable knowledge which can be accumulated, recorded, and transmitted to progressive generations of learners regardless of context (Scribner and Cole, 1973). In this scenario, high status knowledge is provided by schools and universities, with non-institutional learning, such as apprenticeship, relegated to the informal category. The claim of useful knowledge being acquired through non-formal practices in communities of practice (Engeström 1999, 2001; Lave and Wenger, 1991) has only in recent decades gained credibility. Sfard (1998) challenged the use of only two paradigms or metaphors – the behaviourist/cognitivist or the situative practice – claiming that they are both interdependent, and that tensions in the discourses are counter-productive.

The social purpose of education and learning was found by the LSDA researchers to be significant in how different theorist viewed the relative importance of both formal and non-formal learning. Formal learning could be viewed as reproducing the values and norms of a middle class elite (Bourdieu and Passeron, 1990), while informal learning could be viewed as happening at the margins, and in workplaces where dimensions of unequal of power reinforced dominant ideologies (Billett, 2001). The researchers suggest that the recent EU interest in non-formal learning may be rooted in a desire to widen participation opportunities, or, it could be viewed as a risk for marginalised groups who may have the social capital of their own networks colonised and weakened, thus further marginalising them.

Eraut (2000) distinguishes among informal, implicit learning and tacit knowledge, and rejects the notion that informal learning is the residual element when formal learning is excluded from the context. He further advises against the use of the term 'informal;' as it connotes discourses of dress, behaviours and diminution of social differences. Eraut defines personal learning as cognitive reasoning that a person brings to a situation which enables her to think and perform. This includes both implicit knowledge and tacit knowledge, public knowledge and private knowledge. This knowledge, according to Eraut, is not solely individual, but distributed and socially constructed by many people. Eraut categories informal learning into implicit learning, reactive and deliberative learning. He argued from his empirical research into work-based learning, that there are context factors and learning factors at play. Context factors can enable learning by providing structures, relationships and motivation for learning. Learning factors include challenging work, feedback and self-efficacy.

Eraut's conceptualisation of learning factors at work

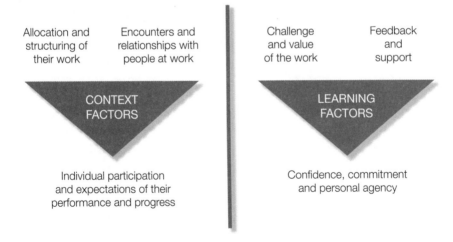

Source: Eraut, UTS Conference *Researching Work and Learning*, December 2005 Sydney.

148

Here, the complexity of any site of informal learning is further exposed and accepts the assumptions that adults do learn from their workplaces, with the nature of that learning contingent on many contextual and temporal factors.

Why a Mindful Search for a Good Theory?

Clearly there are many co-habiting discourses and perspectives competing for dominance regarding the nature of work-based learning, some with more critical awareness than others. The conclusion that the locus of learning and knowledge creation does not reside in the academy, even if the public legitimation of different kinds of knowledges may still reside there, has been reached and generally accepted in critical scholarship of higher education (Salomon, 1993; Coffield, 1998; Garrick, 1998; Symes and McIntyre, 2002; Boud and Solomon, 2003; Rainbird, Fuller and Munroe, 2004; Hodkinson and Hodkinson, 2004). How the academy should respond to this conclusion is the subject of contemporary debates nationally and internationally at the levels of both policy and practice (Boud and Garrick, 1999; Bennett, Dunne and Carré, 2000; Portwood and Costley, 2000; Murphy 2004; Murphy and Fisher, 2004; Nixon et al., 2006) with increasing interest in how learning happens extra-murally in the world of work and how academics are theorising the nature, quality and extent of that learning in order both to understand it and to maintain an element of control over its legitimation. Control over public legitimation of knowledge remains a significant power when types of knowledge are tightly bounded within disciplinary borders, within physical sites and within particular hierarchical conceptualisations of learning. However, as the most powerful knowledges are becoming increasingly generated and controlled by the world of work the traditional practices and theories of the academy can no longer exercise sole power, or perhaps even fully understand how such learning happens when viewed through the lens of traditional pedagogies and academic judgements. A mindful quest for a more expansive understanding of learning at work is now required, both to understand the nature of experiential learning in order to relate it to academic paradigms, and to inform the design of programmes with and for the world of work. Such an expansive understanding is being urged by scholarship from the borderlands between the traditional academy and the workplace (Salomon, 1993; Boud and Solomon, 2003; Illeris, 2004; Billett, 2004) seeking theories which can both accommodate the traditional paradigms and elaborate the complexities of contemporary understanding of learning from work in the world. Mindfulness about learning from work as an approach to theory seeking begins, not with meta-theory, but with practices at the locally constructed and locally negotiated levels. Mindfulness takes cognisance of issues of human agency embedded in everyday actions and interactions of people in their work-related roles and contexts as well as framing such issues in their historical context of labour and production (Engeström and Middleton, 1998, pp.1&2). Mindfulness is more than the cognitive activity and rational planning associated with Cartesian dualism, however. Mindfulness is associated with an acceptance of the potential of human agency in a historical context and includes the human actions of remembering, reasoning, seeing, learning, imitating, sharing, in an overall temporal, if transient, context of social intelligences where cognition is distributed between individuals and between humans and artefacts (Engeström and Middleton, 1998, pp. 1&2). Work practices in mindful analysis are regarded as essentially communicative practices where personal and private mental processes are located in the wider shared, or public, socially and culturally mediated practices.

Accepting that learning through work is a form of mindful practice colours the possible analytical frameworks the academy may use to theorise learning by worker-learners as well as how curricula, syllabi and pedagogies for work-related programmes are understood and acted upon. Using traditional frames of understanding and traditional theories of learning at work is unlikely to enable understanding of the interactions of individual cognition, shared cognition, contexts, artefacts, objects and technologies, distributed at the immediate, local level. A revised theory of learning, or set of theories, is now required to understand the complexities of the knowledge-based society.

Traditional and Emerging Theories of Learning

Hagar (1999a, 1999b, 2000, 2001, 2003, 2004) argues that traditional theories of learning, which are generally favoured by education and training practitioners and which influence further and higher education curricula and pedagogies, are being rapidly displaced by emerging theories of how learning actually happens. In the traditional, or standard, paradigm assumptions about learning remain largely unchallenged. Among the unchallenged assumptions is the acceptance of the body/mind dualism which assumes that learning is a solitary process, that learning activity is primarily individualistic and that it can only be measured at individual level where the learner is somehow aloof from the world. As a result, the most valued form of learning focuses on things, on concepts and on propositions, rather than on minds and bodies immersed in a world of actions. Knowledge that is universal, stable and transmissible is favoured over local, transient knowledge that is situationally responsive. The traditional paradigm regards knowledge as transparent and responsive to accurate recall. Failure to recall accurately indicates a failure of learning. Learning that is tacit, transient or context dependent is less valued in the traditional paradigm. Learning that is favoured resides in individual minds, is propositional, can be expressed verbally for measurement, impacts on cognitive practices, distinguishes between process and product, can be applied to the external world, and is transparent to the mind. This general paradigm influences traditional academic processes, rationale for learner selection, assessment mechanisms, and pedagogical approaches. It favours the notion of universal, context free truths that are transparent to others and which will endure over time and place.

Hager argues that the pace of change in work practices and sites of knowledge production has made the traditional paradigm of learning unsustainable and that there is now accepted scepticism about fundamental truths as well as increasing blurring of certainties between what is individually known and residing in individual minds and what is collectively shared and distributed among persons and artefacts. In particular, the decline of the traditional paradigm questions the status of academic judgement of knowledge as outcome rather than as process, and questions the sustainability of distinguishing between theory and practice as separate elements of the learning act.

The emerging paradigm favours analysis of learning as action in the world, changing both the learner and the environment in a specific time and specific context. Hagar (1999a, 2001) draws on Dewey and Wittgenstein to emphasise the significance of social contexts, activities and objects. Likewise Billett (2004), Boud (2004), Illeris (2004) and Eraut (2005) respectively emphasise the affordances, and the milieu of workplaces in framing an understanding of both the process and product of learning at work, emphasising the shared nature of learning, know-how and the production of new knowledge in any work environment. Boud in particular stresses the significance of productive reflection among workers in generating collective knowledge (Boud, 2004). Likewise O'Connell (2006) theorises the nature and extent of social learning by apprentices with references to the limitations of Vygotsky's zones of proximal learning which give undue weight to external agency and the significance of technologies.

The principles of the emerging paradigm of learning in work emphasises a belief in the capacity of individuals to act in the world, to make judgements and to share knowledge with others. The principles include an acceptance that not all tacit knowledge shared among persons can be made explicit, verbalised or written down for the purpose of judgement, and that it is not always possible to distinguish theory as an entity apart from its application in practice. Judgement, in the emerging paradigm, then, needs to be holistic and integrated, avoiding dualisms of mind/body, theory/practice, thought/action, process/product, knowing that/knowing how. It accepts that propositional knowledge is a subset of learning, but that such knowledge is not always timeless, independent transparent and capable of transmission. The new paradigm regards both propositions and judgements as immersed in the world and not purely transcendental (Hager, 2000).

It could be argued that the standard paradigm of learning is unsympathetic to how learning happens at work and indeed chooses not to engage with the possibilities inevitable in the emerging paradigm. This lack of sympathy and engagement may indicate a reluctance to accept the consequences of the emerging paradigm for academic practice in general and for disciplinary knowledge in particular. It could also be argued that there are differences of pace among disciplines in their understanding and willingness to acknowledge the emerging paradigm. Disciplines which are moving towards an understanding of the complexity of learning in the workplace suffer little anxiety in designing learning programmes by work-based learning contracts, or in using collaborative and participatory pedagogies. Such paradigms regard understanding of how prior learning from work is theorised as essential in designing new programmes where work-based learning is central.

Implications for Adult Education Traditions

Two questions arising from acceptance of the mindful, emerging paradigm of learning are as follows: how does this paradigm sit within adult education traditions? and: will the emerging paradigm effect any change in the academy? In relation to the first question, we could use the schema devised by Tennant (2006, p. 130) as an analytical framework and augment it to include the dimension of the emerging theories of learning in the workplace. In this way we may have an indication of how the liberally, critical and postmodern traditions of adult education, as described by Tennant, might respond to the emerging paradigm of learning. Tennant argues that the field of adult education in the mid-1990s was characterised by chaos and disorder and that it has since become even more fragmented as a discipline in an increasingly complex academic and social world where risk, change and uncertainly predominate. He attributes the chaos and disorder to structural changes in society resulting from globalisation and from the proliferation of information technologies, which together, are requiring renewal and reformation of personal identities. He also attributes it to the foregrounding impact of lifelong learning policies, and to the postmodern intellectual movement which regards diversity, difference and multiple identities as inevitable in contemporary society, as opposed to the apparent cohesion, convergence and singularity of identities in both the personal and public spheres which characterised the modern era. Following Tennant, there may some analytical merit in augmenting Tennant's schema, and in conceptualising how the traditions of adult education – the liberal, humanist and postmodern – regard the individual learner, learner needs, knowledge production, access and equity, relations with 'teachers', as Tennant conceptualised them, and the augmented categories of *views of knowledge and learning, and implications for the emerging theory of learning through work*. However, this is not to presume that any higher education provider is fully aware of its tacit, or implicit, stances with regard to the subtleties of the elements in the matrix. Nor does it presume that the matrix captures the full range of possible position. But it is, nevertheless, a useful point of departure in beginning to articulate a whole-organisation wide philosophy of experiential learning generally, and of learning in the workplace specifically (Geoghegan/Murphy, 2006).

Essentially, a higher education operating from a liberal-humanist stance will be facilitatory, but will remain internally unchallenged both with regard to its legitimation of knowledge or adaptation of the curriculum. A provider operating from a critical theory stance will be conscious of its power control of knowledge, and will respond to challenges posed by the emerging paradigm of learning both structurally and epistemologically. The postmodern provider will be flexible and accommodating, seeking links with society and the work of work. While it could be argued that the liberal-humanist, critical theory, and postmodern stances are philosophically different, it is not clear within which the emerging paradigm of learning would thrive most, and within which it would make the most impact on the internal world of the university. The augmented matrix suggests that we are in the postmodern moment where epistemic opportunities are affording opportunities for redefinition of what constitutes adult learning in an age of super-complexity. The challenge for providers, following this logic, is to recognise the potential in that moment and to mindfully consider how it will respond to the shift in knowledge production away from its own world and to the world of work. The locus of control of learning will inevitably shift from the individualistic, prescribed and acquisitional mode of the traditional paradigm to the collective, non-prescribed and participatory mode of the emerging paradigm, as tentatively suggested in the illustration below.

Control of Learning: traditional and emerging paradigms

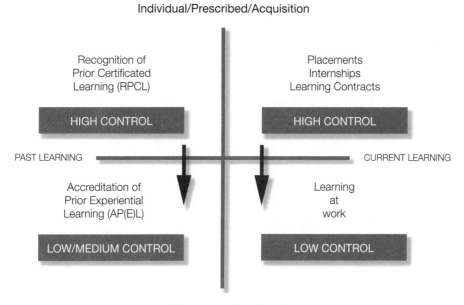

Individual/Prescribed/Acquisition

Recognition of Prior Certificated Learning (RPCL)		Placements Internships Learning Contracts
HIGH CONTROL		HIGH CONTROL

PAST LEARNING ———————————————— CURRENT LEARNING

Accreditation of Prior Experiential Learning (AP(E)L)		Learning at work
LOW/MEDIUM CONTROL		LOW CONTROL

Collective/Non-prescribed/Participatory

The challenge for higher education in the immediate future, then, is to mindfully seek to understand the emerging paradigm of learning through work in relation to its own frequently unquestioned assumptions about the permanence of its own powerful role in knowledge production, and how its traditional structures, policies and pedagogies may be no longer sustainable in a changing world of knowledge production.

Dimensions of three adult education traditions

Adult education tradition	View of self-directed learning	View of learner needs	Access and equity dimension
Liberal Humanism	Learners determine and plan their own goals. Learning is the responsibility of the learner.	Adult education must meet the expressed needs of learners.	Open access is desirable. Individuals are responsible for seeking out access opportunities.
Critical Theory	Autonomy and freedom is not achieved just by mastery. Traditional adult education is class and gender biased. Learners should critique social and cultural power structures.	Individual learners do not always have a means to express needs. Individual needs may not coincide with group or community needs. Needs-meeting provision is akin to commodification and marketisation.	Self-selection widens the gaps in society with a bias towards white, male, middle-class, literate adults. Barriers exist for non-traditional adult learners. HE policies should pro-actively encourage participation by all.
Postmodernism	There is no constant self. The self can be re-interpreted. The autonomous self is aware of its situatedness.	Needs analyses are not necessarily identifying real issues. Language, history and culture should be the objects of critical enquiry.	Structural issues of access are not problematised. The discourse is about diversity rather than equity.

Source: Based on Tennant (2006, p.130) Table 9.2 with augmentation in italics.

Relationship of the 'teacher' and adult learner	View of knowledge and learning	Implications for the emerging theory of learning through work
The teachers is an empathetic facilitator with genuine, non-judgemental concern for the learner. Conflict is avoided. Individual freedom is paramount.	*Academic constructs of knowledge and learning as both a process and a product remain unchallenged.*	*WBL theories are likely to be related to HE current curricula and pedagogies even if the agentic potential of the individual is acknowledged.*
There is a dialogue of mutual trust. The teacher challenges assumptions, often causing discomfort. Teaching and learning are collaborative and the learners have a right to challenge and intervene.	*University knowledge is defined by the powerful and at the expense of the less powerful and indigenous. Real knowledge emerges from both individual effort and collective endeavour.*	*Accepting theories of collective and distributed learning requires higher education and professional bodies to reconsider how professionals learn through work, how they are assessed and how they are accredited.*
Meanings are influenced by context and culture. Meanings are not fixed. The teacher acts as a challenger and decoder of meanings. There is no fixed value set or definitive truth.	*Knowledge is contextual, temporal, collaboratively produced and individually interpreted.*	*Learning is regarded as emerging from life and work experiences with underpinning social learning theory. This links APEL and WBL theory as a continuum in how pedagogies are managed.*

References

Beckett, D. & Hager, P. (2001). *Life, work and learning: Practice in postmodernity.* London: Routledge.

Beckett, D. & Hager, P. (2000). Making judgements as a basis for workplace learning: Towards an epistemology of practice. *International Journal of Lifelong Education*, 19(4), 300-311.

Billett, S. (1998). *Learning in the workplace: Strategies for effective practice.* Sydney: Allen and Unwin.

Billett, S. (2001). Critiquing workplace learning discourses: Participation and continuity at work. Available in the informal education archives: *http://infed.org/archives/e-texts/billet_workplace_learning*.

Billett, S. (2004). Learning through work: Workplace participatory practices. In H. Rainbird, A. Fuller & A. Munro (Eds.), *Workplace learning in context.* London: Routledge.

Boud, D. (Ed.). (1998). *Current issues and new agendas in workplace learning.* Adelaid, Australia: NCVER.

Boud, D. (2001). Knowledge at work: Issues of learning. In D. Boud & N. Solomon (Eds.), *Work-based learning: A new higher education?* London: SRHE.

Boud, D. (2004). The 'elusive' learner and productive perspectives: Linking workplace learning research to practice. Key-note address at the International Research Conference: *Workplace learning: from the learner's perspective*, Learning Lab. Denmark.

Boud, D. & Garrick, J. (Eds.). (1999). *Understanding learning at work.* London: Routledge.

Boud, D. & Solomon, N. (Eds.). (2003). *Work-based learning: A new higher education?* London: SRHE.

Bourdieu, P. & Passeron, J.C. (1990). *Reproduction in education, society and culture.* London: Sage.

Coffield, F. (Ed.). (1998). *Learning at work.* London: ESRC & The Polity Press.

Colley, H., Hodkinson, P. & Malcolm, J. (2003 & 2004). *Non-formal learning: Mapping the conceptual terrain: Consultation report.* London: Learning and Skills Development Agency.

Commission of the European Union, (2001). *Towards a European qualifications framework for lifelong learning*, Brussels: EU.

Commission of the European Union (2004). Principles and guidelines for recognition of non-formal and informal learning. Documents from the Irish presidency, Dublin 2004.

Davis, B. & Sumara, D. J. (1997). Cognition, complexity and teacher education, *Harvard Education Review*, *67*(1), 105-125.

Edwards, R. (1998). Flexibility, reflexivity and reflection in the contemporary workplace, *International Journal of Lifelong Education*, *17*(6), 372-388.

Engeström, Y. and Middleton, D. (Eds.). (1998). *Cognition and communication at work.* Cambridge: Cambridge Press.

Engeström, Y. & Middleton, D. (1998). Studying work as mindful practice. In Y. Engeström & D. Middleton (Eds.), *Cognition and communication at work.* Cambridge: Cambridge University Press.

Engeström, Y. (2004). The new generation of expertise: Seven theses. In H. Rainbird, A. Fuller 7 A. Munro (Eds.), *Workplace learning in context.* London: Routledge.

Eraut, M. (2004a). Transfer of knowledge between education and workplace settings. In H. Rainbird, A. Fuller & A. Munro (Eds.), *Workplace learning in context*, London: Routledge.

Eraut, M. (2004b). Informal learning in the workplace. *Studies in Continuing Education*, *25*(2), 247-273.

Eraut, M. (2005). Learning in the workplace. Conference symposium paper from *Researching Work and Learning*, UTS, Sydney, December 2005.

Fenwick, T. (2002). *New understanding of learning at work: A report at the conclusion of a Coutts-Clarke research fellowship*, Canada: University of Alberta.

Garrick, J. (1998). *Informal learning in the workplace: Unmasking human resources development*, UK: Routledge.

Geoghegan, B./Murphy, A. (2006). *From personal to public learning: Philosophical, policy and pedagogical challenges of AP(E)L in higher education.* Unpublished PhD thesis, NUI Maynooth.

Hager, P. (1999a). *Know-how and workplace practical judgement.* Working Paper 99-01, Sydney: UTS Research Centre for Vocational Education and Training.

Hager, P. (1999b). *Making judgements as the basis of workplace learning: Preliminary research findings.* Working Paper 99-02, Sydney: UTS OVAL.

Hager, P. (2000). *Conceptions of learning.* Working Paper 26, UTS OVAL Research.

Hager, R. (2001). *Towards a productive conception of productive learning.* Working Paper 01-13, Sydney: UTS Research Centre for Vocational Educational and Training.

Hager, P. (2003). *Changing pedagogy: Productive learning.* Research Working Paper 13-16, UTS: OVAL.

Hager, P. (2004). The conceptualisation and measurement of learning at work. In H. Rainbird, A. Fuller & A. Munro (Eds.), *Workplace learning in context.* London: Routledge.

Hodkinson, P. & Hodkinson, H. (2004). The complexities of workplace learning: Problems and dangers in trying to measure attainment. In H. Rainbird, A. Fuller & A. Munro (Eds.), *Workplace learning in context.* London: Routledge.

Illeris, K. (2004). *Learning in working life.* Denmark: Roskilde University.

Kincheloe, J. (1999). *How do we tell the workers? The socioeconomic foundations of work and vocational education.* Colorado: Westview Press

Lave, J. & Wenger, E. (1991). *Situated learning: Legitimate peripheral participation.* Cambridge: Cambridge University Press.

Lynch, K. (2006). Neo-liberalism and marketisation: The implications for higher education. *European Educational Research Journal,* 5(1).

Murphy, A. (2004). Situated learning – Distributed cognition: Do academics really need to know? *Level3* DIT on-line journal, (2nd ed.).

Murphy, A. & Fisher, S. (2004). From a re-active to a pro-active model of work-based learning: Implications for a higher education institute. Conference paper *Work-based learning from the learner's perspective*, Learning Lab. Denmark, Copenhagen, December 2004.

NQAI, (2005). *Principles and operational guidelines for recognition of prior learning in further and higher education.* Dublin: NQAI.

Nixon, I., Smith, K., Stafford, R. & Camm, S. (2006). *Work-based learning: Illuminating the higher education landscape.* York: Higher Education Academy.

O'Connell, E.K. (2006). *Social learning on the job: An analysis of the socially enabled learning of apprentice electricians*, Unpublished Masters thesis, Dublin Institute of Technology.

Portwood, D. & Costley, C. (2000). *Work based learning and the university: New perspectives and Practices.* London: SEDA.

Rainbird, H., Fuller, A. & Munro, A. (Eds.). (2004). *Workplace learning in context.* London: Routledge.

Rogoff, B. (1990). *Apprenticeship in thinking.* Oxford: Oxford University Press

Ryan, A. (2001). Challenging the gatekeepers of knowledge, Proceedings of HEEU Conference, Maynooth.

Salomon, G. (Ed.). (1993). *Distributed cognitions: Psychological and educational considerations*, Cambridge: Cambridge University Press.

Schribner, S. (1985). Knowledge at work. *Anthropology and Education Quarterly*, 16, 199-206.

Sfard, A. (1998). On two metaphors of learning and the danger of choosing just one. *Educational Researcher*, 27(2), 4-13.

Symes, C. & McIntyre, J. (Eds.). (2004). *Working knowledge: The new vocationalism and higher Education.* London: SRHE.

Tennant, M. (2006). *Psychology of adult learning.* (3rd ed.). London: RoutledgeFalmer.